PATTAYA

'Patpong on Steroids'

Duncan Stearn

Mitraphab Press

Mitraphab Centre Pty Ltd
24 Davies Street
Kincumber, NSW 2251
Australia

First published by Mitraphab Press	March 2002
Reprinted	October 2002
Revised and Updated	September 2003
Revised and Updated	October 2004

Cover design and layout by Duncan Stearn

Also by Duncan Stearn:

The Ultimate Accolade (New South Wales Greyhound of the Year Title 1965-1985)

Chronology of South-East Asian History 1400-1996

Pattaya Unplugged

Pattaya Snaps, A Celebration of the Women of Pattaya
(with David Kuri)

Acknowledgements

My thanks to Mike and Janet Sheedy who first brought me to Thailand; little did they realise just what an affect the place would have on such a delicate wallflower as me.

Thank you to Chris Grsic, Gary Morley, Neville Pick, Peter Culpan, Colin Hastings, Peter Noldus, and Rob Norris among others who took the time to read parts of the manuscript and earlier versions of the book and offer their thoughts.

I would also like to thank the many people who purchased the first few editions of the book and made it one of the most popular in Thailand. In particular I would like to thank those who made the effort to contact me with their impressions and comments about the book. I hope this further revised edition will be met with equal favour.

"Do not be afraid of going slowly, only of standing still."
-Chinese proverb

Contents

Preface

This book was originally compiled and written over a period of five years and deals primarily with the Thai resort city of Pattaya, especially its ubiquitous sex trade.

Much of this book concentrates on specific incidents and events that happened to me, as well as a few friends and acquaintances, while living in Pattaya and travelling around Thailand. Entwined with this I have included what I consider appropriate and relevant statistical and historical information in the hope of putting some of these incidents into perspective. To this end, the book is a combination of travelogue, social commentary, and autobiography.

Thailand and Pattaya in particular, has an alliterative rhapsody of searing sun, sparkling sea and sensual sex whose magnetic allure can prove as irresistible as the legendary Sirens who taunted and tempted a brave Ulysses.

The chapter entitled 'The Ugly Australians' is a behind-the-scenes account of an attempt at character assassination by Australia's leading current affairs program, *60 Minutes*. Much of the chapter appeared as an article in the Bangkok-based *The Big Chilli* magazine in April 2001.

The damage to my reputation and that of many others who come to visit Thailand and particularly the resort centre of Pattaya has been done and, in the closed and narrow minds of many thousands of gullible people, can never be restored no matter what we say or do.

Nevertheless, it is my belief the majority of people want to know the truth and hear both sides of an argument before passing final judgement. That is the aim of the chapter: to provide the truth as I believe it to be and to present an alternative argument to the one presented on Australian and New Zealand nationwide television by *60 Minutes*.

Thailand has been described as "the most sensuous spot on earth", and I will readily admit to being seduced by the country and its people, in spite of a few unfortunate occurrences and incidents, including death threats.

The country possesses a soporific charm that transcends logic and it continually lures people from all walks of life into its illusory and idyllic embrace. This is true of so many foreigners who leave behind their past lives and tread a well-worn path to the Land of Smiles. Very few people, and not just the so-called 'sex tourists', visit Thailand just once in their lives. It's that kind of place.

One person who succumbed to Thailand's charms was the now-deceased Jeffrey Bernard. Well known for his columns in the English magazine *The Spectator*, he wrote, in an April 1995 edition, about his sponsorship- via the Christian Children's Fund of Great Britain- of a young girl in Thailand. *"Her name is Sum. Apart from any concern as to her health and safety in the area where she lives, which is at times infested with Cambodian bandits, and whether or not she is by now working in a massage parlour in Bangkok, it would make, I think, a very good story were I to go out there to meet her and see for myself...I would like to see Sum, just to see if the piddling amount of money she gets from me -about two large vodkas a week- has been of any benefit to her...When I was last in Bangkok, I was assured that young Thai women will do anything, but anything, for you if you ask them nicely. If this is true then the temptation to take advantage would be so evil it doesn't bear contemplation."*

Despite all good intention those comments would have served to merely reinforce the Western stereotyping of Thai womanhood in the minds of many of his readers.

The bulk of tourist experience in Thailand is limited to tours of places like Bangkok, Chiang Mai, Phuket, and Koh Samui as well as Pattaya, Trat or Hat Yai.

The average person will spend a couple of weeks travelling about in hire cars, air-conditioned buses or trains, unable to speak more than a few words of Thai and generally looking at the sights and sounds on the well-worn tourist trail before returning home with an impression of a country of smiling faces, spicy foods, enervating humidity, temples and vibrant nightlife.

Even backpackers rarely experience a true village atmosphere, and as they tend to travel in pairs or larger groups, do not get to interact with the locals on anything more than a desultory basis.

For that matter, many foreigners work on contract in the country, sometimes for lengthy periods, and leave with not much more than a rudimentary knowledge of the nation and its people.

This is not meant as a criticism, merely an observation. After all, our experiences of most countries are always limited to the amount of time and money we have to spend in them and the intercourse- both sexual and otherwise-with the locals.

In this book, I have tried to remain as impartial as possible in my discourse, but there is always a judgement- or bias- implicit in writing what one perceives as the truth. Perhaps some will see my views and attitudes as some form of hidden agenda designed to justify and enhance the international sex industry in Pattaya. Nothing could be further from the truth. I am merely presenting the reality as I have experienced it and hope my comments will be seen as fair and reasonable.

While the girls who ply their trade to foreigners generally do so willingly, it is a willingness brought about primarily, and generally, by the desire to improve the overall financial lot of themselves and their families. In recent times, it has been noticeable that many of the younger women entering the sex trade are simply too lazy to find employment in more demanding and less rewarding positions. It's easier and more lucrative to work out of a go-go bar or simply freelance in discos and nightclubs for customers.

Thailand is not a welfare state and so individuals within the family group meet the burden of providing for the family. It is common to see grandparents shouldering the burden of looking after their grandchildren while their daughters and sons seek employment away from the village in the major cities and towns.

I hope my love for this region and its people will come through the pages of this book and if it goes some way to helping understand the nature of prostitution in Pattaya then it will have been a success.

Note on currency

I have refrained from converting the various amounts of Thai Baht, Lao Kip, Cambodian Riel, and other currencies mentioned in this book into equivalent amounts in Australian or US Dollars. The reason is simple. When I first went to Thailand at the end of 1993, I received just over 16 baht to the Aussie Dollar. In early 1998, I obtained 30 baht for the same Aussie dollar during the fallout of the Asian economic crisis of 1997. The variations in currency from one year to the next will only serve to confuse the reader as to the real worth of a particular monetary unit. If I feel the need to make a comparison with another country's currency I have done so and hope the emphasis placed within the text is clear enough as to whether an item is cheap or expensive. Note that all dollar references are in United States currency unless otherwise stated.

1

In the Beginning

Like a Virgin

Never before, and not since, I first came to Thailand, and the hedonistic paradise of Pattaya in particular, have I felt more at home in the world. For a long time I have believed the twists and turns of fate, both good and bad, all happen for ultimately positive reasons. This belief, though I wasn't aware of it until I came to Thailand, is reflected in the Buddhist theory of *karma* (the law of cause and effect), and it was this that led to my first trip to the country in November 1993.

At the time, I was a semi-professional gambler working the horse, harness and greyhound racetracks of Sydney. In that capacity, I was acquainted with a wealthy punter nicknamed 'Long Pockets'. He was a regular customer of well-known bookmaker John Waterhouse, who, because he had trouble remembering the names of many of his clients, used nicknames to differentiate them. 'Long Pockets' was so named because of his propensity to keep producing larger and larger amounts of money to put on horses, pacers, and greyhounds.

Over a period of time I came to know 'Long Pockets', whose real name was Mike. A regular at the greyhound races at Wentworth Park in Sydney, he would frequently sidle up to me and ask, "Do you like anything tonight?"

My *karma* was right as I managed to tip him five consecutive winners over a period of three meetings, all winning at good odds, and making Mike a lot of money.

Mike was married to an attractive and friendly lady from Thailand, a country I knew little about. Early in our acquaintance he'd asked, "Have you ever been to Thailand?"

"No," I replied. "It's not a place I've ever thought about visiting."

I'd only heard about Bangkok's infamous Patpong Road from an American girl who worked at a cafe in Kings Cross. She claimed the place was, in her words, "wild." Even then, I knew nothing about Thailand's infamous go-go bars and its media-fuelled reputation as a sexual haven.

"You should go one day, I think you'd probably like it, especially if you like Asian girls," Mike explained.

Then one night during this winning streak at Wentworth Park he said, "I've won a lot of money backing your tips. We're going to Thailand soon and I'd like to give you the airfare so you can come with us."

I thanked him for his kind offer but did not accept. My friends told me I was crazy not to go, so when he offered a second time, I accepted. Thus was the die cast.

Mike and his wife Janet (her Anglicised name; her Thai nickname is Deuan), his brother Tony and a friend named Leo were going to Thailand about three weeks after he made the offer. Mike organised the visa and bought the plane tickets; all I had to do was front up at Sydney airport on the day of departure.

***

Perhaps the first thing that struck me was the size of Bangkok's Don Muang International airport. It made Sydney's Kingsford-Smith International Terminal look like a provincial weigh-station.

Although the name 'Don Muang' sounds suspiciously Spanish and could easily refer to a nobleman banished to the wilds of Asia for conduct involving jars of Vaseline and underage boys, it simply describes the location of the airport rather than conferring a memorial like La Guardia in New York or Charles de Gaulle in Paris.

Along with Singapore, Bangkok is a gateway to Asia and a major stopover point for travellers commuting between Europe and Australia and the southeast Asian region.

The airport is huge, one of the largest and busiest in the world, and getting busier. After our plane landed, it seemed to take an eternity to taxi to its designated parking space in the terminal. It took so long I thought the pilot was treating us to a special tour of the various runways.

Once outside the air-conditioned terminal the first thing that hits you is the heat and humidity. It is oppressive, but then what else would you expect being just one centimetre away from the Equator, that is if you're looking at a map of the world.

There was also a pungent aroma that can only be described as a mixture of decaying, wet vegetation (mainly the incredibly odious Durian fruit), dried fish, and spicy cooking odours blended with a liberal dash of exhaust emissions, small waste fires and uncovered sewers. It is the essential smell of the southeast Asian city and Bangkok can rightly claim prime position at the top of the aromatic tree.

After finding a bus or a taxi to travel into the city it quickly dawns on you Don Muang airport is closer to the capital of Mongolia than Bangkok. A trip from Sydney to Wollongong on a retarded donkey would at times be quicker than traversing the clogged streets from Don Muang to central Bangkok, although the advent of the Skytrain in late 1999 made travel around some parts of Bangkok almost pleasurable.

The contrasts between Thailand and Australia were glaringly obvious almost from the moment I stepped off the plane. Contrasts I found agreeable, interesting and enjoyable. After all, I come from a country where foreigners have asked me if it is true that kangaroos and emus are to be found roaming the thoroughfares of cities like Sydney and Melbourne. It's almost cruel to see their faces drop when you disabuse them of this notion. Yet, in Bangkok and Pattaya, I have seen elephants swaying majestically along the sidewalks and down traffic snarled arteries while their mahouts offer curious onlookers bananas to feed the hungry beasts. No wonder I fell in love with the place.

***

Thailand has a population of over 65 million people (most seem to live in Bangkok), around 75 percent are ethnic Thai while some 14 percent are Chinese-Thai, the latter group being pretty much in control of everything from politics through to business.

It is a country of striking natural beauty and man-made eyesores; of vibrant, happy, smiling faces and a murder rate amongst the highest in the world; of serenity and peaceful ambience juxtaposed with bacchanalian excess; where the mendicant travel side-by-side with the affluent; where noise is a virtue, and a cacophony of sounds assaults the senses and rarely abates in daylight hours.

The first word most foreigners hear in Thai is *farang*. Meaning foreigner it's not usually used in a pejorative fashion and, similar to other Asian cultures, the Thais have difficulty with the 'r' and 'l' sounds of the English alphabet, the word comes out as 'falang'.

An old Thai chronicle observed that *farang* were very tall, hairy, and evil smelling but the females were quite beautiful, despite the fact they were large and round. The chronicle concluded with the matter-of-fact statement, *'they do not grow rice.'*

The Buddhist religion is embraced by around 95 percent of the population and it is Buddhism, allied with entrenched animist superstitions, which shapes much of the Thai cultural make-up. To gain any measure of understanding about Thailand and Thai people it is necessary to study Buddhism- more a way of life than a dogmatic religion- and the importance of 'merit making'.

Like Christianity and Islam, Buddhism has devolved into sub-sects and in Thailand it is of the Theravada strand, sometimes referred to as Hinayana- or 'Little Vehicle'. It originated in southern India; its canon is in Pali (a chanting that sounds like people who've been on medication with serious side-effects) and promises the bliss of reaching Nirvana (heaven) following many incarnations. Doing good deeds, ostensibly out of the goodness of one's heart rather than the thought of personal gain, is what makes 'merit' and the road to Nirvana sees one start off as something akin to a sewer rat and finish up, after a series of incarnations, as a man, before finally entering paradise.

There is a saying in Thailand that women are the 'hind legs of the elephant'. Loosely translated it means women are subordinate in every way to men. Theravada Buddhism only serves to confirm this belief, as a woman is considered to be a rung or two down the reincarnation ladder, behind male taxi drivers, male homosexuals, and male politicians, although not necessarily in that order.

Buddhist monks have to be registered and usually number around 275,000. In one particular year, 192 were arrested for misconduct for offences ranging from being guilty of intoxication, asking for merits without permission, staying in people's residence, gambling, sexual abuse, and being ordained illegally.

Becoming a monk does not take a so-called 'calling' from God. As a part of the framework of life, it is expected most Thai men will spend time as a monk. Some join for as little as three months while others stay for life. Criminals, some on the run from the authorities and others who have completed their jail sentences, quite often become monks.

A Thai taxi driver, who concocted a story about finding a vast amount of money in his cab, returning it intact to the foreign owner and then receiving only a pitiful reward, was convicted of fraud and sentenced to jail. His false story had reached the papers and people sent him about 200,000 baht as compensation for his goodness, all the while gaining 'merit' for themselves. When he was convicted of the fraud, he said he would become a monk on his release. Either that or he may be given the finance portfolio in the Thai government.

***

Thailand's reputation as the Land of Smiles can be somewhat misleading in a country with a high murder (over 5,000 people in 2000) and suicide rate, a stratified society and a streak of racial intolerance common to all races across the world. For example, an old Thai proverb states, "If you are out walking and meet a cobra and an Indian, kill the Indian first."

Yet, the Land of Smiles appellation, in general, is a true reflection of the nature of the people and the ambiguity of Buddhism. The average Thai lives for the day- there is no grieving over past mistakes or concern for the imponderable future. In general, they enjoy sex and are not burdened with a sense of shame or guilt about it. Buddhism has imbued the people with a wonderful *joie de vrie* that encompasses everyone from the humblest rice farmer to the most powerful corporate executive. They have a great sense of humour as well as an ability to accept the hand life deals for them. Thai women are considered among the most beautiful in the world, a claim I would not even consider disputing.

I have often found it somewhat incongruous that every brothel, massage parlour, go-go bar, and beer bar has a Buddhist spirit shrine and many of the girls, before going onstage for their turn to dance topless, will solemnly *wai* the Buddha.

The *wai* is a prayer-like gesture in which the hands are clasped together and raised in front of the face for a brief second or two. When Thai people greet each other it is usually with a *wai* and because of the strict class structure of society, the 'inferior' will *wai* his or her 'superior' first. Of course, the trick is to know who is superior to whom.

It is also fascinating to watch a hardened go-go girl come into a bar before it is open to the public armed with soft drink, oranges, and other items, and place them ceremonially on the shrine while removing the old offerings. She will then burn incense and pray for a minute or so in front of the shrine. Who knows what she may be praying for but my guess would be something like, *'oh Lord Buddha please grant me an easy short-time with a very wealthy and generous farang tonight.'* She will then *wai* and proceed to change into her working attire, which usually amounts to not much more than a g-string.

Buddhism is also reflected in a ritual I have seen performed in a go-go bar that may be struggling for customers. In one, a girl dressed only in a black bra and g-string, removed her top, held a glass of water between her hands and silently prayed in front of the shrine. After about a minute or so, she ran around the centre stage four or five times holding the glass of water aloft. This action completed she returned to the front of the shrine, prayed briefly again and put her top back on. In some countries she would have been hauled off to a mental institution and sedated with large needles.

In another bar, a similar ritual is performed, but to make it even more personal the dancing girls take a single hair from their pubic region and add it to the glass. I just hope they remember to wash the glass thoroughly afterwards.

All this sounds like some form of ceremony you'd expect to see in a Masonic lodge, complete with funny handshakes and leather aprons. Instead, it happens in go-go bars and is performed in the hope Buddha will intervene and bring plenty of willing customers to the bar so the working girls can be taken out for sex.

Although female prostitutes might be ashamed of their trade, it is not seen as so great a deviation that they fall outside the embrace of Buddhism.

Despite the ostensibly mendicant nature of Buddhism, the conspicuous flaunting of money and power is a key element in the Thai psyche. Money signifies status, and status is paramount in society. The more money you have, the higher the status. Considering a significant percentage of the population live in conditions of poverty, especially in the northeast (a region known as Isaan), it is not hard to understand the importance placed on money.

How material wealth is obtained is of little concern to the majority of Thais. The fact you have it is enough to suggest your *karma* was right and you deserved it, even if you happen to be the local mafia boss or successful prostitute. From the lowliest police constable to members of parliament, the process of wealth accumulation and its methods are accepted with a typical Thai phrase, *'mai pen rai'* (basically translated as 'never mind'). This is colloquially claimed to be the national motto.

For example, an article appeared in the 10 April 1997 edition of the *Bangkok Post* about a sleepy little village by the name of Ban Jan, located in Roi Et province. The village, according to the reporter, could easily be mistaken for a modern housing estate in Bangkok. The place is full of dwellings ranging from 'airy two-storey teakwood houses to staid European mansions...' The reason Ban Jan was so affluent, especially when compared with its neighbouring villages, was it had acquired the cognomen of the 'Swiss village'. For the previous 15 or so years, many of the girls from the village had been going to Switzerland to work as call girls and dancers on eight-month contracts. The money they earned in that time was usually enough to set themselves and their families up in style. The fact everyone knew what was happening was immaterial, as long as the girl was successful. In fact, many of the women

Is this the quintessential Pattaya T-shirt? Seen on a mannequin in one of the many shops selling cheap clothes. The four-letter word seems appropriate for almost everyone who comes to Pattaya for a ‘good time’.

were married to Thai men before deciding to go and work in Switzerland.

Nonetheless, there is a price to pay. Divorce rates are high; many of the girls stay on in Switzerland and marry Swiss nationals; the men of the village, so used to being pampered and taken care of by their women, don't work and spend their days drinking, playing snooker and gambling.

As a Professor of History was quoted as saying, "It's easy to condemn the villagers of Ban Jan, but as long as our society keeps bleeding the poor dry and giving them few opportunities in life, it is difficult to stop what the villagers believe is the only way to get themselves the good life."

A girl who leaves the rice paddies of her poor village, heads for the bright lights of Bangkok or Pattaya, takes on the role of glamorous courtesan, and manages to send back enough money to substantially improve the economic conditions of her impoverished parents is regarded as successful. Even the status of the girl's parents will rise considerably in the village. That a new house and relative wealth were accumulated via a daughter plying the world's oldest profession matters not a jot. When she has made enough she may well be in a position to go back to her village, marry, and be accepted. Were she a corporate raider she could gain no higher respect within the village; success is its own reward.

***

In 1965, just 250,000 tourists travelled to Thailand, yet by 2004, over 10 million visitors a year were making their way to the country and staying for an average of seven days, making Thailand the number one tourist destination in southeast Asia. The money generated is the largest source of foreign exchange.

A large number of the visitors to Thailand are men (many of them single, or married men travelling without their wives) and sex for money is a key tourism ingredient. If there is any truth to feminist writer, Rana Kabbani's statement that, 'one travels to exercise power over land, women, peoples' then maybe Thailand, and especially Pattaya provides a compelling example.

The exotic Orient has always proved a powerful sexual magnet. Travel writing, by both men and women, since the early 19th century has done nothing more than reinforce the stereotype of Asia as some form of sexual paradise. The writings of such luminaries as Joseph Conrad, W. Somerset Maugham, and Graham Greene certainly went a long way to reinforcing this stereotype.

Sadly, the foreign media is largely responsible for portraying Thailand as a land of nothing more than prostitutes and illicit drugs, with a few temples thrown in for good measure. Most written accounts dealing with the sex industry in the country seem to be moralising tracts seeking to impose perceived superior Western mores on a culture and people viewed, obliquely if not openly, as racially inferior.

Despite their engaging smiles, most women in Thailand exude an air of *noli me tangere* and there are many women running highly successful businesses.

***

This was all unknown to me as we checked into the Pattaya U Hotel, located in a quiet *soi* (as the side streets are known) in north Pattaya. The rooms were spacious, carpeted, air-conditioned with good hot water showers.

Each morning we travelled from the Pattaya U down the Beach Road to south Pattaya partaking of a hearty breakfast of bacon, eggs, baked beans, sausages, and toast as well as a mug of tea or coffee at the Anzac Hotel (now Lewiinski's). The incongruity of this was not lost on me. We had spent some nine hours travelling by jet aircraft over 7,000 kilometres only to eat the same food we could have ordered just down the road from our respective front doors in Australia.

As I was soon to learn, many Thai cooks are definitely not used to cooking in the Western style. Take a simple item like toast. A toaster is a cooking utensil that remains a source of wonder for most Thai chefs. If you order a couple of slices of toast you are likely to receive bread that looks as though it's been threatened with being placed into the toaster rather than actually having experienced the sensation. The cooks wave the bread in the general direction of the toaster and then threaten it with usage. Most toasters in Thailand must rust out rather than wear out, a phenomenon that surely baffles manufacturers.

The Anzac, as the name implied, was a meeting place for Australians and New Zealanders as well as catering to a large English clientele. It had a well-worn blue-felt pool table, a sizeable television and video (mainly featuring movies of the action genre), the walls were adorned with old World War One prints showing Anzac troops in action at Gallipoli and on the Western Front and was spacious enough to accommodate around eight good-sized dining tables.

Mark, an Englishman and Tony Brady, an Australian, ran the hotel in partnership. Tony was short of stature and lean with slicked-back dark hair. He reminded me of Humphrey Bogart, with gravel voice to match. Most days he would be found standing in the corner of the bar nearest the street, reading the *Bangkok Post,* doing the cryptic crossword and smoking a million cigarettes while complaining about the precarious nature of the business in which he was engaged.

I became friendly with Na, one of the waitresses working at the Anzac. She was 21-years-old and worked six days a week, from 8:00 a.m. until 4:00 p.m. For this, she earned about 2,000 baht a month, of which she paid 1,500 baht a month in rent. Therefore, she and the others working in the Anzac relied on tips from customers to make any real money.

Na was very popular as she had a nice face, a ready smile and a quiet personality. When I returned nine months later she had left the Anzac and I was told she'd married an Englishman.

Na was typical of many of the girls who didn't work in bars. They came to work in hotels and restaurants as receptionists, waitresses, maids and cooks and generally hoped to find a good foreigner who would marry them.

Some, envious of the money and good hours kept by bargirls, eventually found their way into the sex trade, while others were attempting to get away from the business and start a new and more respectable life. Still others had foreign boyfriends who paid them not to work in the bars anymore and instead find employment in a more respectable, if less monetarily rewarding, profession.

Patpong on Steroids

Pattaya is viewed as a kind of modern day Sodom and Gomorrah in some quarters. Nevertheless, every weekend the roads from Bangkok to Pattaya are clogged with Thais leaving the polluted, gridlocked capital and heading to the resort. Some even wind up in the go-go bars normally frequented by foreigners.

Well over 2 million people visit Pattaya each year, and the largest percentage are Thai nationals. Tourists from the People's Republic of China, Taiwan, Korea, Japan, Germany, and Britain make up the majority of people visiting Pattaya from outside Thailand, although increasing numbers come from Russia. The Severe Acute Respiratory Syndrome (SARS) outbreak of early 2003 briefly saw an enormous decline in tourists coming from northern Asia, clearly exposing the fragility of the tourist mix away from the bar scene. The desire to promote north Asian tourism into Pattaya, resulting in overloading the streets with gargantuan tour buses belching enough diesel fumes to dissolve the ozone layer, may have been seen as an easy way of making a lot of money for the city. However, the profile of visitors such as these means (a) very few repeat customers and (b) an easily deterred demographic.

Located about 150 kilometres on the coast southeast of Bangkok, Pattaya has gone from a nondescript small fishing community in the 1950s to something more substantial during the years of the Vietnam War (1964-1975) before starting to gather tourist pace in the late 1970s and 1980s. It is easy to forget that Second Road was only paved in late 1992, not long after the opening of the Royal Garden Plaza shopping centre. Large shopping malls like Tesco-Lotus and Carrefour hung out a shingle from the late 1990s onward.

American troops stationed in Thailand during the Vietnam War were sent to build an airstrip at U-Tapao- just down the road from Pattaya- and some would spend their leisure time (R&R) on the beach or travel out to Koh Larn (an island neatly located on the outskirts of Pattaya Bay) with the local fishermen.

Wherever there are lonely servicemen with wads of spare cash there will be women, and soon bars and guesthouses began to spring up in the fledgling town.

In 1978, it was raised to the status of a city. Although it now offers all the kinds of typical tourist attractions you would expect of a resort, Pattaya is still the largest open-air brothel in the world and, despite efforts to the contrary, this is what continues to draw the majority of visitors.

For most of its life Pattaya has been seen as the almost exclusive playground of the so-called 'sex tourist'. The city fathers set about trying to change overseas media perceptions with a series of fairly successful campaigns aimed at attracting 'respectable' tourists, such as couples, families, and the corporate and convention market. Right at the end of the last century, efforts by the local government to improve Pattaya's image abroad began to pay off as increasing numbers of families and couples started to make their presence felt. In some cases this may not be as innocent and wholesome as it appears. Reports in the British media in 2004 suggested there were an increasing number of young, and not so young, British ladies travelling to Pattaya with the avowed aim of paying to get laid by Thai boys working in the bars. I am certainly aware of a few European ladies of not-so-tender years regularly scouring the bars in search of new conquests.

Almost from the beginning, Pattaya has suffered bad press, not all of it unwarranted. Claims town planning was a joke of over-building, that its hotels had contributed greatly to pollution in the Gulf of Thailand and threats by travel agents across three continents to boycott the resort due to claims of over-charging failed to stop international tourists flocking to the place.

The long-awaited waste treatment plant at the south end of Pattaya Bay was completed and brought on line at the end of 2000 with the result that the bay became cleaner for swimming for the first time in a couple of decades.

***

The respected American writer Stan Sesser claimed the most dangerous thing he ever did in southeast Asia was try to cross the street in Bangkok. Beach Road and Second Road in Pattaya are not much different.

In most countries of the world, a zebra crossing is an invitation to the perambulator to exert a measure of authority over that metallic monster, the motorised vehicle. Ordinary citizens will stride forth onto a zebra crossing, confident the magical properties of these man-made road etchings will grant them immunity from a fatal or injurious collision with on-coming vehicles. Zebra crossings are, in the minds of many, like an invisible force field, providing instant protection from bodily harm, no matter what the circumstance. This is not so in southeast Asia, and most definitely not in Pattaya.

Unless you happen to be an elephant, trying to enforce the rights of a pedestrian on a zebra crossing should be left to the clinically insane or suicidal. Even if you are an elephant, using a zebra crossing will increase your chances of being ploughed into by a motorbike or car.

So why have the city fathers deigned to provide them in the first place if they are not meant to be used by pedestrians? Is it some kind of twisted joke? 'Let's mark out those silly Western-style pedestrian crossings and see how many tourists are stupid enough to try and use them.' Are hospitals and doctors really in need of that much business and medical practice?

Perhaps the government once mistakenly signed an international treaty calling for the introduction of pedestrian crossings on roadways, thinking instead they were agreeing to the sale of pachyderms for work in Zimbabwe. When they discovered the truth, they could hardly say they'd made a mistake and pedestrian crossings wouldn't work in Thailand. 'By the way, what's a pedestrian?'

In Bangkok the authorities long ago realised the free flow of the motor vehicle was far more important than that of people who got around on foot.

In the stifling heat of Bangkok, only poor people, mad dogs and Englishmen actually use their legs for such a mundane an activity as walking. Everyone else is either driven around by a chauffeur (the incredibly rich, politicians, and leading gangsters), drive his or her own car (business people, and up-and-coming gangsters), catch a bus, taxi or tuk-tuk (most of the rest).

So, since people who walk obviously enjoy exercise, the authorities responsible for maintaining traffic jams very thoughtfully built outdoor Stairmasters so pedestrians could not only cross the road but they could increase their heart rate and more aerobic activity into their daily routine.

These Stairmasters are cleverly marketed as pedestrian overpasses and consist of two flights of stairs, each of up to 800 steps and guarded at various points by decrepit looking people disguised as beggars, followed by a bridge over the roadway beneath and then a corresponding set of two flights so you can work your lower calves as you descend to the other side.

Of course, for people in wheelchairs, the elderly, the blind, the incredibly overweight and young children under the age of five, these Stairmasters are not recommended.

Pattaya has yet to build a single pedestrian overpass across either the Beach or Second Road's, but the time cannot be too far away when it will happen, simply because zebra crossings are wonderful in an ordered society where everyone understands exactly what they are for, but not in the traffic maelstrom the resort has become in recent years.

In Pattaya, trying to do the chicken thing (get to the other side) is becoming an increasingly dangerous activity not to be undertaken by anyone with a serious heart condition, an injury that makes rapid movement difficult or who is over the age of 50 and carrying more girth than the average Sumo wrestler. Although, in the latter case this is not so catastrophic as most vehicles will mistake you for a blundering pachyderm and make every effort to avoid a collision that could be fatal to them as well as you.

Hoping for a gap in the traffic is probably what inspired Samuel Beckett to write his famous- and exceedingly boring- play *Waiting for Godot.* Indeed, I've waited so long to try and get across Second Road on some occasions that the local male mongrels, thinking I'm some form of human sculpture, have contemplated using my legs for their three-legged water ballet.

Just try fending off a bunch of mongrels while edging out into oncoming traffic and dodging a flying Kawasaki Boss, Honda Dream or the wonderfully named Suzuki Smash, and you will understand why the sooner the city erects an overpass the better.

***

The roads, especially after heavy rain, sometimes feature potholes rivalling the size of moon craters. The sidewalks are generally uneven or non-existent and, as with Bangkok, the smell of exhaust fumes hangs heavy in the air. The whitewashed buildings of the city look exactly like the whitewashed buildings of every other Thai city and after a few years start to get that grey-stained appearance, with chips and cracks surfacing.

The samlor, the notoriously unstable noisy three-wheeled scourge of Bangkok (known generally as the tuk-tuk) has thankfully been barred from plying the streets of Pattaya. Instead, Pattaya has dozens of songthaews, colloquially known as Baht-Buses.

Imagine a dark-blue utility with the rear tailgate down, a step attached to the tailgate to permit access, bench seats on either side of the tray and covered over the top to keep the sun off your head and you have a baht bus.

From close observation, most of the drivers of these diesel-belching machines are quite mad. But then, if you spent your life driving up and down and around and around in circles all day every day just to earn the price of a chicken and rice dish and drinking large quantities if Lipovitan (a concentrated caffeine liquid equivalent to 50 cups of coffee per bottle), you'd be quite loopy as well.

At a set of traffic lights (where the average waiting time for a colour change gives a female enough leeway to apply a trowel-load of makeup, eye shadow and lipstick) it is not uncommon for a driver to test the efficacy of his smoke emissions by applying one foot firmly to the accelerator while the other remains on the brake and then checking to see how many passengers he's managed to render unconscious in the baht bus drawn up alongside him.

One baht bus in particular seemed determined to hasten the onset of global warming with a sterling contribution in diesel exhaust emission. His vehicle had obviously suffered some form of terminal malfunction that allowed the engine to keep running, but was insufficient to give the vehicle itself much forward velocity. So, in what I think was the vain hope forceful application of the accelerator would lead to a miraculous cure, the driver pressed the pedal to the metal and managed to get his vehicle to crawl at snail pace around the next corner, whereupon it shuddered to a halt. The process led to the emission of more smoke than the average malfunctioning Russian power station could belch out in a calendar year and made the Chernobyl meltdown look like a staff barbeque.

From the late 1990s onwards, traffic along Beach and Second Road, especially at weekends and during the high season, can be as clogged as Bangkok, making it faster to walk than drive a car or ride in a baht bus.

***

Perhaps the real test of a resort is the number of fast food franchises- the majority of which began life somewhere in the United States in places with obscure names like Hog Bottom, Minnesota and started by people with improbable cognomens such as Colonel Hiram Stinkfinger III- that hang out a shingle or two in those resorts.

In this regard, Pattaya must rank among the king of world seaside resort towns, because just about every fast food franchise ever devised by man and inflicted upon the unsuspecting and gullible public of this planet seems to have at least one outlet in the city.

Food in general is relatively cheap at the hundreds of street-side stalls and small cafes, but for those who cannot handle the spicy Thai food they need never go hungry.

The Royal Garden Plaza complex, stretching between Beach and Second Road, houses a large number of shops where tourists can buy just about anything their heart desires. Just when they need that little fillip to give them the spurt to go on shopping till they drop, the Beach Road end of the Plaza has a phalanx of fast food joints all waiting to serve you a speedy culinary masterpiece.

Pattaya local car wash. This photo was taken not more than 10 minutes drive out of Pattaya.

You want a Big Mac, we've got McDonald's; you like the look of Colonel Sanders, well just across the way is KFC, complete with a life-size model with hand outstretched in greeting at the entrance. For all I know it may well be the embalmed body of the Colonel, fully preserved in 23 different herbs and spices. Then there's Burger King and the Pizza Company (formerly Pizza Hut, but that's another story) to complete the front rank of the franchises.

Just in case you think you can sneak the ankle-biters out the back and get away scot free, the all-you-can-eat-until-you-explode Sizzler restaurant is waiting to lure you through its portals. The place is a favourite with the steroid heads who make Pattaya their training village and they can be observed launching a gastronomic massacre against the salad and soup bar.

Then there's Starbucks, Swensen's, Au Bon Pain, and others all within a five-minute walking radius of each other. Fast food was never so fast or easy to obtain.

When I first came to Pattaya there didn't appear to be many really good quality restaurants. By the turn of the century Pattaya was fortunate enough to see the establishment of a large number of quality munching dens, stretching across the city from the south to the north. The prices at some of these places are high by Pattaya standards, but still relatively cheap by European.

In an effort to bring a little bit of that feeling of 'home', a number of entrepreneurs constructed the kinds of bars and restaurants that would not be out of place in Bilious-on-Sea, Yorkshire, Pigswill, Georgia, or Hamburgernschtuffen, Bavaria.

Places such as the Pig N Whistle, Rosie O'Grady's and Shenanigans (no prizes for guessing that the former is a replica English boozer while the latter pair roughly equate to places you might strike in the less salubrious parts of Ireland).

There's also Henry J. Beans, a restaurant and bar picturesquely set in an old colonial mansion of the kind extant in the days of the American Civil War in the Confederate south. Very *Gone With the Wind*, although the modern day Clark Gable is apt to be an overweight retired accountant from Hump Springs, Kansas and Scarlett O'Hara's real name is Nok and she's working to feed her six-year-old daughter who's back in her village of Barn Yai Kwai, Udon Thani.

One of the truly great edifices about town is the Hopf Brew House, a replica of a giant German beer hall. Walk past here and you think oompah bands, beer steins and lederhosen. Walk inside and you get an Italian tenor, yard glasses (full of freshly brewed beer) and not a hint of leather gear.

So far, no one has yet set up a replica of an Australian outback pub (the Three Urinals) or a Mongolian yurt, and I'm fairly certain the climate here is not conducive to an imitation igloo. This may have more to do with the fact that genuine Eskimos are a bit thin on the ground in these parts.

Most restaurants catering to a foreign clientele offer a standard English or American-style breakfast. Actually, the term breakfast is a bit of a misnomer, as most ex-pats and tourists seem to develop nocturnal habits, so most of the time 'breakfast' is closer to 'lunch'. That is, by the time most people have arisen from their slumbers, the sun is high in the sky and the early birds are already lining up tomorrow's worms.

In fact, anybody foolish enough to start wandering around the town between the hours of 7:00 a.m. to 8:00 a.m. could be forgiven for thinking the place had been decimated by a mysterious plague, as there is hardly anything or anyone moving.

In most cities of the world, office workers and building labourers are out of bed just after dawn, preparing to meet yet another day, but Pattaya, despite having plenty of offices and businesses other than bars and restaurants, tends to remain somnolent until late morning.

About the only time anything of any note does happen is once a year when the runners in the Pattaya Marathon listen for the sound of the starter's gun at the ungodly hour of 5:00 a.m. In 2001, there were no less than 10,000 participants in the marathon, half-marathon and quarter-marathon, including Peng Perngsa, an 87-year-old man who hailed from Ratchburi and was recognised as the oldest man running marathons. He took up the sport at the tender age of 78. I'll be lucky to be able to move around in a Zimmer frame at 78, let alone take up running.

***

Pattaya has overdosed on shops, markets and stalls selling almost anything made on the planet. The Thais are among the best copiers in the world and good quality ersatz shirts, T-shirts and jeans, name brand watches, pirate videos, cassette tapes, CD's, computer games and software can be obtained somewhere along the beach front or the Second Road. It is even alleged false passports and identities can be had in certain saloons and shops about the town.

The four floors of the Mike Shopping Mall have anything and everything for sale and seem to have more employees per square metre than any department store I have ever seen. The employees appear to spend most of their time applying and re-applying their make-up; staring for hours at tiny mirrors while picking at the most minute portions of their face; dozing with heads resting on folded arms; sitting and staring into space or chatting with their workmates while eating. And that's just the men.

However, it is the bars and the women for which the resort is infamous and to which it owes its very existence.

Pattaya is Patpong on serious steroids. While the Patpong bars and go-go's cover just three small streets in the capital, Pattaya has over 600 bars that could be described as aimed primarily at foreign tourists. These are staffed by upwards of 10,000 girls.

A stroll down Walking Street (formerly known as the Golden Mile or The Strip) in south Pattaya is like entering a garish Dante's Inferno. The Walking Street is a collection of beer bars, go-go's, restaurants and shops where multi-coloured neon lights burn brightly over many of the bar entrances. The street is usually clogged with tourists- predominantly men- ambling from bar-to-bar, shop-to-shop or restaurant-to-restaurant. All the while they are exhorted and cajoled by hawkers and barkers to come and sample the delights of Happy Hour in the multifarious boozers.

When I first came to Pattaya, cars and motorbikes were permitted down the road, adding to the melee. Now the street is closed off to traffic from 7:00 p.m. until 2:00 a.m., thus earning its appellation of Walking Street. Indeed, it has become such a well-known tourist attraction that during the high season (from about November through until February) the place is packed with people doing exactly that, walking. Unfortunately, some of the bar owners complain that is all the tourists do, walk. They don't stop in the bars for a drink, and those who do only tend to stay for the one libation before trekking off yet again.

The only other area comparable to Walking Street is Pattayaland Soi 2, a five-minute saunter away. When I was first in Thailand this *soi* had just one go-go bar, called The Classroom. A few years later it was lit-up like a giant Christmas tree with some 10 go-go bars as well as beer bars along its length. By 2003, the go-go's of Walking Street had made a resurgence and the number of go-go's in Pattayaland Soi 2 had been reduced to eight.

***

There are also those who make a living, not from working in the bars, but by selling products to the customers of the bars. From the early evening until the wee small hours a motley collection of people of all ages hawk almost anything and everything at the outside beer bars.

Young children-many of them illegal immigrants from Burma and Cambodia, some homeless or parentless-roam through the bars with trays of chewing gum and sweets for sale. They descend like a plague of locusts every night on the multitude of beer bars throughout Pattaya, tugging, generally forlornly, at the shirtsleeves and elbows of drinkers sitting at the various bars, trying, usually with mournful looks or engaging smiles, to sell their wares for 10 or 20 baht. The children range in age from five or six up to around 14 or 15 and are on the streets until 2:00 or 3:00 a.m. as they go from bar to bar.

Older children and men wander through the bars sticking packs of cigarettes under your nose with a monotone, "Marlboro"- the brand of choice for so many Thais. At the outside beer bars this ritual can occur 40-50 times during the course of a night, becoming more annoying than blowflies at a barbeque.

The nightly throng of lolly, chewing gum, cigarette, cigarette lighter, wallet, stuffed toy and flower sellers have their ranks swelled by snake-handlers (both the python and green tree variety), iguana peddlers, photographers, shoeshine boys and beggars, who all compete with the bargirls for the attention of the hapless foreigner wrapped around his drink.

One of the dancers who used to work in the old Caligula's Palace a-go-go in *Soi* Diamond. It is now known as Super Girl a-go-go.

The World's Oldest Profession

Prostitution, despite being officially illegal in the Land of Smiles, hardly leads a clandestine existence. In his *World Human Rights Guide*, Charles Humana stated, "the failure of the government to exercise law or reduce poverty has created a sex trade estimated to involve 1% of the population, so distorting normal family life." Using Humana's figures, out of a population of around 65 million people, some 600,000 are involved in some way in the sex industry, either full-time or part-time. The Children's Rights Protection Center estimated 2 million females earned a living from the sex industry, and some 800,000 of these were children under 16 years of age. In May 2003 one national newspaper claimed there were 32,113 prostitutes working in the province of Chonburi; in October that same year, a rival newspaper stated there were 24,608 people engaging in the world's oldest profession in the same province.

The true size of the industry undoubtedly lies between the various figures and does not detract from Humana's statement about the distortion of normal family life. The numbers of children- particularly in rural areas- being brought up by grandparents while their mothers attempt to carve out a decent living is disproportionate by any standard.

Despite the exodus to the cities, most people still live in rural villages, planting rice and growing just enough food to live. To have any understanding of the sex trade and its impact it is necessary to eschew Western mores and look closely at rural Thailand- the breeding ground of the industry. What these girls can earn via prostitution in a relatively short space of time is generally more than their parents will have earned in their collective lifetimes.

An International Labour Organisation (ILO) study concluded prostitution "...has become an integral part of the Thai economy..." and nothing is likely to change "...while the cost incentives remain the same, and the opportunities for alternative employment are so limited." The ILO estimated around 500,000 people made their living via prostitution.

The girls who make up the majority of sex workers dealing with foreigners usually have extremely limited educational qualifications (generally not much more than primary school) and, because of their darker skin (mainly girls from the northeast) and leaner bodies are not considered attractive enough to work in Thai-frequented bars.

One of the reasons why so many of the working girls have Thai boyfriends is the foreigners they meet are, to quote one outspoken girl, "boring. They [the foreigners] get drunk and we have to sit and listen for hours as they tell is their endless problems." Most Thai men, apart from the obvious language and cultural familiarities, go to bars to enjoy themselves and this factor alone makes them more appealing than most foreigners.

Although bargirls do wind up getting married to foreigners, for many of the girls it's not for that ethereal thing called 'love' but security. One girl said, "When we start getting past the age of attraction, and meet a man who is halfway decent and responsible, we marry him. It's a matter of life security [not] romantic love."

Indeed, one bar owner told me, "I've had a number of girls who have had two foreigners wanting to marry them. One is old, fat and rich and the other, almost invariably, is young, handsome and poor. The girls obviously really like the young guy but they ask my wife what they should do, and she just tells them they have to look after their future. In all the cases the old, fat, rich guy wins out."

That varying cultures can and do exhibit different attitudes towards sex and single women can be gauged by the difference between the age-old customs of the Iban (or Land Dyak people of Sarawak in Malaysia) as well as a place like modern Spain.

The Iban people lived communally in a longhouse. James and Charles Brooke, the late 19th century British white rajahs of Sarawak, found the uninhibited sexuality of longhouse life more than merely intellectually intriguing. A young Charles Brooke would visit a longhouse and find himself, as a single man, invited to the bed of any young lady who took his fancy. This was an Iban custom whenever single men came to visit. Charles wrote that he found Iban women attractive and sexually inventive lovers. If he decided to take a woman as a mistress, it was easily organised. When he grew tired of her and decided to take someone new, the woman could return to the longhouse to marry, her status enhanced rather than detracted by having been the mistress of a man of Charles' status.

In some districts of Spain as well as other Western European nations, it is quite common to see sex workers engaged in casual conversation with both customers and prospective clients out on the streets of local suburbia. This style of sex work, mirrored in many ways by the bar scene in Thailand, makes working conditions more conducive to developing friendships, and even long-term relationships, with clients.

For some women in the industry, regular clients can become friends and the boundaries between their private and working lives begin to shift and become blurred. This is something which happens on a regular basis and is even more pronounced in the international bar scene in Thailand. In fact, the girls here tend to consider themselves as 'rented wives', not mere 'prostitutes'. It may be playing at semantics, but the difference is important.

Prostitution in Thailand is not the product of Western influence. Prior to the abolition of slavery in 1905, prostitutes came from the ranks of women in the slave market. They were sold as either slave women or slave wives. The former would be forced to perform sexual favours for other men as well as her master while the latter belonged completely to her husband. The abolition of slavery led to an increase in the numbers of women involved in prostitution, as former slaves had nowhere else to go. Thai society promoted polygamy and to this day still tacitly accepts- but does not condone- the concept of *mia noi*, or 'minor wives'.

From 1905 until 1960, prostitution was legal and controlled under the Venereal Disease Control Act of 1909 that established a system of licensing for brothels and prostitutes. The Act stated girls must be at least 15 years of age and could not be forced into the business against their will. Illegal prostitution nevertheless continued.

When Marshal Sarit Thanarat seized power in 1958, he paid 'coup money' to the generals who helped him take power and provided opportunities for them to make money by land speculation, smuggling and other enterprises.

In response to international pressures, the sex industry became an obsession with Sarit and he worked to eliminate it. However, for all his posturing Sarit had no less than 100 women as mia noi in a supreme act of 'do as I say, not as I do'. When he died in 1963, he was found to have embezzled over 400 million baht, most of it spent on his minor wives.

Those young ladies were not averse to spending time with other men, as the biography of New Zealand-born, United States-based journalist Peter Arnett attests. Arnett recalls the time he spent in Bangkok as a young up-and-coming journalist and mentions an assignation with one of Sarit's minor wives.

A 1960 paper published by the Ministry of the Interior claimed 90 percent of prostitutes were aged between 15 and 20 and they averaged five clients per night. That same year, after the number of northern girls becoming prostitutes grew at an alarming pace, the government introduced the Suppression of Prostitution Act, banning the industry. Like most places in the world, it continued relatively unchecked. Instead, it became the preserve of the underworld.

Shortly after the banning of prostitution and opium smoking, the first massage parlour (a former opium den) opened on Bangkok's Silom Road. Since then, massage parlours have spread across the country like feral cats on speed.

The sex industry first came to international prominence in the decade after the end of the Second World War and by the late 1950s, overseas writers and journalists, most spending just a few days or weeks in the country, had begun writing about the seedy underbelly of life in Thailand.

Back in the 1950s and 1960s Bangkok earned a reputation as the world's pornographic film capital and strip clubs hired European girls to take off their clothes for randy patrons, both Asian and foreign. Bangkok was labelled by some as the most immoral and corrupt city in Asia. Even inveterate American traveller Paul Theroux fell into the trap of describing Bangkok merely as a city of 'temples and brothels.'

According to Professor Cohen of the Hebrew University, "Tourism...had a crucial impact on the [prostitution] trade. Not only did the number of girls engaging in prostitution grow considerably, but also the nature of the occupation changed with the emergence of the new clientele. The interaction with white, foreign, male tourist farangs engendered a new subculture of prostitution."

Nevertheless, in spite of Bangkok's onomatopoeic reputation as a centre of sex-tourism, the majority of working girls ply their trade in places frequented by natives.

Perhaps one of the reasons for Thailand's growing reputation as a virtual repository of glorious vice was the fact its people were far less likely to feign moral indignation than their Caucasian counterparts. There is openness about the sex for sale industry that can make it appear far larger and all consuming than it really is.

For many Thais sex is just another bodily function, not an act of which to be ashamed. Sex is not considered 'dirty' or something to be talked about in hushed tones. Even among the higher strata of society, jokes with a latent or even overt sexual theme are hardly discouraged or frowned upon.

Between 1965 and 1966 while the number of go-go bars, massage parlours, and other illegal sex dens in Bangkok more than doubled, yet kissing on television was not permitted and it was scandalous for men and women to be seen caressing or even holding hands in public. In up-country villages it was taboo for a man to touch a woman in public.

In 1966, the Thai government passed the Entertainment Places Act to control nightclubs, dance halls and bars in the hope of reducing the sex industry. It continued unabated.

In 1967, Thailand agreed to play host to United States service personnel who came on R&R. At the time there were already thousands of troops scattered throughout the country in a number of US-run bases. Within three years, the Americans were spending the equivalent of 25 percent of Thailand's annual rice export and Bangkok quickly confirmed its mantle as the sex capital of southeast Asia.

Sociologists claimed the lure of relatively easy money was far too strong for girls who had previously only known poverty. American soldiers, unleashed on Bangkok for a few days of R&R, reportedly fathered more than 2,000 children by 1968 alone. To be fair, the Thai 'Queen Cobra' regiment was doing the same thing in war-torn South Vietnam, where they produced an average of one baby for every 13 soldiers. Talk about being on 'active service'.

***

The Thai are a proud and intensely patriotic people. The national flag of red, white, blue, white and red horizontal stripes flies proudly from every flagpole around the nation. Indeed not only every flagpole, but anything remotely resembling a flagpole, is liable to have the national ensign fluttering atop it. At 8:00 a.m. and 6:00 p.m., all television stations stop to play the National Anthem. Television stations usually conclude programming by playing the National Anthem. It is common to see young schoolchildren sing along with the anthem. Indeed, the school day only starts after the National Anthem has been sung while the flag is raised at morning assembly.

This almost jingoistic reverence bestows upon the country an arcane old world charm, and perhaps the anachronistic Cinema Censorship Code of 1930 helps to encapsulate the dichotomy that is Thailand. Any scenes deemed objectionable are quickly cut from television productions so the sight of naked flesh on TV screens is kept to a minimum and even then confined largely to foreign-made films. Contrast this with prostitution. Despite its illegality, its operations are hardly clandestine and any policeman will smilingly point you in the direction of the nearest 'bawdy house'.

Part of the reason for the easy availability of women- and men- for paid sex can be traced back to the education system, rural poverty and the fact females outnumber males.

Although Thailand boasts an adult literacy rate above 90 percent, the vast majority of children do not receive more than the ostensibly free- and now compulsory- six years of primary schooling between the ages of seven and 15.

Sending a child to school for longer than six years is almost impossible for many impoverished rural families due to the expense involved. Indeed, even attending school for those six years can be impossible for many children. Most rural children are able to virtually take care of themselves (i.e. wash, cook, clean and shop) by the time they are 10 years old and many work in the fields both before and after they come home from school.

One girl, working in a go-go bar in Pattaya, was quoted as saying, "I always wanted to be a doctor, but my family was poor and I couldn't go to school."

Another said, "Do you think I sat as a little girl and thought, 'When I grow up I can go to Pattaya and sell myself to a bunch of dirty old men?'...but when you're poor and have many brothers and sisters and everyone's hungry all the time you do anything to survive..."

In 1965, the American researchers William Masters and Virginia Johnson produced the results of a 12-year survey entitled *Human Sexual Response*. One of the findings of this survey was to debunk the myth all prostitutes were frigid. Masters and Johnson found the second-greatest motivation for becoming involved in prostitution was sexual desire. The first motive, obviously, was economic and it is this that largely fuels both the domestic and the international sex industry in Thailand.

The girls who work in the bars of Bangkok and Pattaya frequented by foreigners do so willingly. They are rarely compelled to go with men they don't like, and usually only in Thai-owned bars or under pressure from the Thai mamasan, and are paid a monthly salary. They are able to leave the bar at any time and go to work elsewhere or return home without hindrance. There are also an increasingly large number of girls who 'freelance' in various bars and tout for business along the beachfront in Pattaya.

Lack of more than a basic education means many women can only find employment in menial jobs requiring long hours for low pay. In the northeast of the country, women go to work in the rice fields for not much more than a subsistence salary. The work is long and arduous and the rewards are limited to sustainability of daily life and not much more. In some cases, sustainability can only be maintained by going into debt. In some cases, money is borrowed from landlords just to purchase enough food to live. For some, prostitution is seen as the only escape route from a life of poverty, squalor and even starvation.

Nevertheless, they choose to work the bars and the streets with many of them, especially the younger girls, not wanting to find permanent boyfriends or husbands. They like the idea of being able to go with whomever they want, whenever they want. They have a freedom and independence they could never hope to replicate in their home villages and towns.

Many of the good-looking girls are quite aware of their physical charms and their attraction to foreign men. They utilise their charms to extract as much money as they possibly can out of as many men as possible. I don't blame them for doing so; a return to poverty is hardly a welcome thought for these girls.

Canadian novelist and former university professor Christopher Moore, a long-time resident of Thailand, stated in an interview with the Bangkok-based magazine *The Big Chilli*:

"...It is nearly impossible to generalize about the sex worker or the customer. There is great comfort in such generalizations but comfort is an illusion as the reality is always often far more noble and far more sordid and terrible. In other words, what goes on in the night world of Bangkok is filled with contradictions.

The Thais are far cleverer than the farang as they are content to live with ambiguity; it is the foreigners who go mad trying to resolve what cannot be resolved. That good and evil, wrong and right, honesty and dishonesty, betrayal and loyalty are mostly blurred, that life rarely renders a clear-cut definition between the extremes and we spend most of our time in the gray areas...We live in an age of Hollywood where complexity is greeted with horror- simple answers, simple images.

It is worth noting an article in the English language newspaper *The Nation* in 1985 recounting the story of 15 hill-tribe girls rescued from prostitution in a Bangkok brothel and sent back home. A few months later the independence, glamour and adventure of the brothel saw them all leave the harsh life of the village and willingly return to work in the brothel.

There are gangs who organise the recruitment and placement of prostitutes and the two most popular countries for Thai sex workers in the late 1990s were Japan and Australia.

The girls are sold by agents to brothels and are told on arrival they owe a large sum of money that can only be recouped by the girls working very long hours in cramped conditions at the mercy of the brothel-owners. Most of the women who come into Japan and Australia to work in brothels travel on fake passports.

In Australia, I became acquainted with a 28-year-old from Yasothon who had been lured from Thailand to work as a bonded prostitute in Sydney. She had been married to a Chinese-Thai man who was killed in a car accident while they were living in Bangkok. She had a three-year-old son at the time of her husband's death and was working in a clothes shop in the Suphan Kwai district when some friends working in the brothel industry told her she could make good money by going to Australia.

After arriving, she was told she owed 30,000 Australian dollars for her bond and a further 5,000 dollars for visa requirements. She spoke almost no English and started work in a Chinese-owned brothel in the inner city. The madam was Chinese and informed her she needed to 'service' 600 clients in order to work off her debt. During that time, she received free food and free accommodation, as well as a few hundred dollars every couple of weeks so she could go out and buy clothes. The brothel, she said, had some 15-20 girls, most of them Asian.

It took four months to work off the debt (at an average of five clients a day) and she then went into a relationship with one of her regular clients. That lasted 18 months and during part of that time she went to work as a dancer at a strip club for four hours a day, two or three days a week. During the whole time, she failed to save any money and in the process became a heavy smoker and gambler, eventually breaking up with her boyfriend and starting work in a Thai-owned brothel. When her visa expired, she remained as an illegal alien rather than return to Thailand empty-handed.

***

One problem that can lead some girls into prostitution is the ID card, or lack of one if the girls happen to be originally from countries like Cambodia or Laos. All Thai residents are required by law to have an identity card. This is a small plastic card with a photo of the recipient on the left. The photo is taken with a height measure as a backdrop and the details on the card indicate the name, birth date (in the Buddhist calendar) and the province from which the person originates.

It is impossible to get legal employment without the identity card. In a country where bribery and corruption is an art form, it is possible to obtain a card that shows, for example, the age of the person as older or younger, as the case may warrant. Although the girls are supposed to be at least 18 years of age to work in bars, there are always some who, with the help of a compliant management, are under-age.

For example, I met a girl named Dai who was visiting a bar in the Best Friend Beer Bar complex. Dai told me she was a dancer at a go-go in Soi Cowboy in Bangkok and when I asked how old she was, she said "18." A few days after this she saw me and said she was actually only 17. She showed me her ID card, which card confirmed her age at 17. Nevertheless, I later found out she was in reality only 15 and that was why she was no longer working in Soi Cowboy. She claimed it cost her just 1,000 baht to falsify her ID card.

Jow was a very tall, attractive girl working in Lightning Jack's A Go-Go who spoke fluent Japanese and Chinese and not really a 'bar-girl' type. She was 28 and had lived in Japan with her Japanese husband for eight years. The union had produced a three-year-old son. She had been in Pattaya for seven months and after working at Lightning Jack's for a couple of weeks I found an advertisement in the *Bangkok Post* for a job requiring a person who could act as a translator in Japanese. I gave Jow the advert and told her she should apply for the position.

"I can't," she told me.

"Why not?"

"I don't have ID card," she explained.

She returned to Thailand when her marriage ended, but had not renewed her ID card. She was hoping to save enough money to bribe someone and obtain a new one.

Jow did eventually save enough money to obtain an ID card and left Lightning Jack's, working as a guide for Japanese tourists.

***

Although every story is unique, there seems to be a basic profile to most of the average working girls, in particular the ones who come to work in beer bars rather than go-go's. The stories vary from girl to girl but the basic paradigm remains constant.

In many parts of Thailand, especially in the rural areas, girls can be living with a man and have their first child by the time they are 16 or 17. Most of the working girls fall into the 18-26-year-old age bracket, have one or two young children and are from the impoverished rural areas of the country (usually Isaan).

The husband/boyfriend has either been killed in a motor vehicle accident or she left him because of his drinking/womanising and her parents back in the village or the farm are now caring for her progeny.

The girl rents a small room for between 1,500-3,000 baht a month, very often sharing with one or two and sometimes more working girls.

When the girls finish with their husbands or boyfriends, they occasionally decide to have nothing to do with Thai men anymore and become part of the international sex trade by travelling to Pattaya or Bangkok in search of a foreigner. They have the illusion that a foreign man will treat them with more respect than a Thai man. When this illusion wears thin, they sometimes again take up with Thai men.

Some of the girls parlay their 'sob' stories into big money from gullible foreigners while others actually play down their sorry plight. They also have a mistaken belief most foreign men are rich. They don't seem to realise most men work hard to save enough money to come to Bangkok or Pattaya for three, four or five weeks each year.

When they first receive 500 or 1,000 baht for a night of sex it is sometimes more money than they have ever seen at one time in their whole life. This economic enfranchisement and, especially for the go-go dancers, the 'glamour' of being the object of men's attention cannot be underestimated.

For many girls their future security becomes entwined with a foreigner from Germany, England, the United States, Australia, or a myriad of other countries. Many a foreigner has come to Thailand, been swept up by its sensuousness and mistaken that sensuality for true love in the form of a girl from a go-go or beer bar.

Initially it is the man, the provider of monetary gain for the girl, who holds the whip hand. In many cases the roles are soon reversed as the girl weaves a certain magic and the lonely foreigner determines to take her from the bar and save her for himself.

As lust turns into the deeper emotion of love it is not uncommon to see the foreigner and his girlfriend go through the motions of a marriage ceremony in his new bride's village, the future prosperity of her parents and family almost assured.

In fact, you sometimes wonder just who really is being exploited. There are many girls who, after working for a couple of years, have two and sometimes three or more foreigners with whom they maintain a relationship of sorts. The best I've heard of is eight men sending money to the one woman. She was at least smart enough to take the cash and buy three beer bars in a prime location in south Pattaya.

The men will come into town for a few weeks or a couple of months at a time and the girls will stop work and go with them. Of course, problems arise when one or more of the men are in town at the same time. That happens a great deal, especially around Christmas and New Year. Usually, the man who is sending the most money on a monthly basis is given preference. The cash cow with the most milk is the one who has to be nurtured.

***

The average foreigner coming to Pattaya tends to be a European man in his late thirties or older, a bit overweight, a drinker with a failed marriage and possibly a couple of kids behind him. It will be his second or third trip to Thailand and he will scour the beer bars and the go-go's for his 'perfect match'.

When he finds a girl that satisfies his tastes he assumes the role of a knight in shining armour, determined after a couple of nights of passion this is the girl for him and he will save her from this life of debauchery by offering to send her money so she can stop working in the bar.

The girl readily accedes to this and quits the bar forthwith. In some cases, the girls take the money and waste it on gambling, usually at cards, or drinking and partying, or giving it to their Thai boyfriends. When the money starts to run short, they will telephone or e-mail their foreign boyfriends and ask for a bit more money. The man is so 'pussy-struck' he can't see beyond the beautiful smile and the gorgeous body and continues to send money. In the meantime, she may still do the odd 'short-time' with men she finds attractive or who offer large sums of money. Thus are the tables turned, and the exploiter becomes the exploited.

As Jeremy Seabrook has written in his book *Travels In The Skin Trade*, "The monetary transaction becomes buried in a haze of emotion. Only when he discovers that he is expected to pay for and help keep many dependants...he becomes swiftly disillusioned. The demands for more money force him to re-evaluate the relationship. Self-righteous anger and resentment come to the surface. He begins to see himself as victim."

In recent years it's no surprise Internet cafes have sprung up all over Pattaya. In a news story the former Hollywood 'Madam to the Stars', Heidi Fleiss quipped, "Call girls don't need madams now, just modems." The girls- and boys- working in the night entertainment industry have embraced Internet technology with a fervour matched only by captains of industry and corporate raiders. A walk past almost any Internet Cafe will reveal a veritable smorgasbord of talent madly tapping away at the keyboards sending messages of undying love, devotion and bank account details into cyberspace.

The days of waiting for the snail mail to deliver a letter replying to desperate pleas for monetary assistance are long gone. Now sob stories concerning retarded buffaloes and the much-needed hospitalisation of near and dear family members can be sent in real time with the replies being almost instantaneous.

Needless to say, not every girl is like this. There are many who have foreign boyfriends and are in receipt of money from them and do in fact stop work and wait until he returns.

I don't blame the girls for getting as much as possible from however many men they can. After all, they are a bit like elite athletes with only a few years at the top of the tree. If they kick off at around age 18 and manage to keep their looks and body in shape they may well have a 'career' in the premier league until about 30. After then pickings tend to become a bit slimmer as the newer and younger 'athletes' take the cream.

As Siriporn Skrobanek of the Foundation for Women said, "In no other country do people expect to establish long-term relationships with sex workers...So what is going on in their head when they meet women in clubs, bars and brothels?"

I disagree with an element of the above statement, in that there are countries where sex workers and clients can and do form relationships (Spain, The Philippines, and the Dominican Republic for example), although admittedly on a far reduced scale than in Thailand.

Nevertheless, it's a bit stupid getting angry with a Thai bar girl for allegedly being ripped off. No one compels foreigners to come to Thailand and get involved physically or emotionally with the working girls or send them money. It's done out of free choice, a modern version of the 'knight in shining armour saving the hapless damsel in distress' and if people get 'stung' it's better to put it down to experience.

***

On my first trip to Thailand, one of the leading go-go bars in Pattaya was a place named Caligula's Palace. It was located in Soi Diamond; a quadrangle with, then, six go-go bars spread down either side with beer bars in the centre and considered the prime location along Walking Street.

Caligula's had around 10 girls dancing on stage at any one time, the majority of them topless and many quite attractive. The first night I went in with Mike, Janet, Tony, and Leo I met a girl named May. She couldn't speak a word of English. We complemented each other, as I couldn't speak a word of Thai.

May was attractive and had been working in the bar a short time, not even long enough to learn any rudimentary English. I think "hello" and "I love you" were the only phrases she had picked up, but then what else do you really need on your go-go bar CV?

When I came back to Thailand some 10 months later I saw her again in Caligula's. She had lost a little weight but looked very fit and had learnt to speak reasonable English.

She told me she had just returned from nearly three months in Germany, where she'd gone to be with her German boyfriend. Unfortunately, the boyfriend had a wife and May returned to Thailand with what she claimed was a "broken heart."

Then 27-years-old, she had become a heavy drinker and smoker. Her seven-year-old son she told me stayed with his father's family.

May later went and had a tattoo done over her left breast. Tattoos have become almost *de rigueur* among many of the bargirls and I have even seen them on so-called respectable females, especially younger girls. Within Thai society a tattoo on a female still tends to classify that person as being of lower class.

A few months later May said her mother had come down from the country and was staying with her. They were sharing a room and paying 3,500 baht a month rent while May earned 5,000 baht a month salary in the bar. She was doing a lot of 'short-times' at about 1,000 baht a throw, so she was making good money.

One night, when she had stopped dancing and was working as a barker for Honey A-Go-Go (just across the road from Soi Diamond), she told me she had an English boyfriend sending her money not to work and an American who had bought her a wedding ring. She had dyed the front of her hair blonde, looked in good shape and claimed she was not doing any short times. I asked her which one she liked and she said the Englishman.

I next saw her when she was the mamasan of a small and ultimately unsuccessful go-go bar in Soi Diamond, next door to her old 'alma mater'. By this time, Caligula's had also closed down after the female Thai owner seemed to lose the plot. It later re-opened under new management and new name, Super Girl.

May eventually married her English boyfriend, but they split up after a couple of years. I ran into her one night in *Soi* 8. Then 33, her hair had been cut back to her shoulders. She'd started work in a beer bar. I asked why she hadn't gone back to the go-go's and she replied, "May old lady".

Within a couple of months, she was back dancing in a go-go. Despite her age, May still managed to get plenty of customers, many of them much younger than her. Later she became a barker for a go-go bar, in Pattayaland Soi 1.

***

On the opposite side of the coin, I suppose it's only natural a town like Pattaya would be home to, and attract, large numbers of people who don't fit the traditional stereotype: married for 12 years, a house in the suburbs, 3.5 children, one dog, two cats, two cars and a hefty mortgage.

It would not be out of order to say some of the foreign men who visit Pattaya are types women in their own countries would generally find unattractive in physical, intellectual or emotional terms.

In polite company the word 'eccentric' is often used for people who are basically borderline mad or, in some cases, have gone completely over the edge but no one's quite noticed yet. The quirks and foibles of some of these people add to the not-quite-on-this-planet air of Pattaya.

For example, there is a man of European extraction (I think one of the Germanic races) who purchased an apartment in a condominium complex and seems to be forever trying to make his unit impregnable to everything but a nuclear holocaust.

He purchased a wrought iron front door and after it was installed, realised it would be possible for people like the Great Train Robbers and characters of that ilk to remove the hinges, gain access and cart off the family silver.

Not wanting to be unhinged (in a door sense, not a mind sense, although there are some doubts in this area) he set about with a blowtorch and drill to add a few more holes for a few extra bolts and then welded the whole contraption so 16 tonnes of dynamite wouldn't be able to prise it open.

Not more than a year later, clearly concerned the potential for home invasion remained a point or two above zero, he again set to work with drill and blowtorch and added metal flaps to encase the said hinges and then, the piece de resistance, installed a set of padlocks.

He now takes about 20 minutes to open his front door to access his fortress. Unfortunately, no one seems to have mentioned the possibility of someone climbing in from outside the building and entering this Pattaya version of Colditz Castle via the balcony.

***

Some men (myself included) claim they prefer the charms of an Asian woman to those of the women in their own country. Although this may be true, there are working girls in Pattaya who feel foreign women are beautiful and, as one girl was quoted as saying, "...the real reason is that these men themselves are not charming enough to attract their own kind. I wouldn't want most of them as a life partner."

Although it does happen that in the early mornings and evenings some foreign men exert themselves by running or jogging along the promenade from south to north Pattaya and vice versa, the majority of foreign visitors and residents seem to invoke Robert Morley's famous maxim, "Whenever I get the urge to exercise I lie down until it goes away."

If you've ever wondered what really happens to the clothes you dump in the local church recycling bin under the cover of darkness, a large quantity winds up on the backs of foreigners who both live in and visit Pattaya.

There are men whose dress sense appears seriously retarded. Many look like they get dressed with the lights off, as pictures of sartorial elegance they are not. Either that or there are a number of strange secret societies extant in the town or a multitude of 'bad taste' parties held every night of the week. Men whose idea of casual dress includes wearing short white or black socks and sandals, with knee-length baggy trousers, tatty singlets, all designed to complement bad comb-overs.

I once saw a tall man with shoulders the size of cement trucks sauntering down Sukhumvit Road in Bangkok dressed in a bright- and by bright I mean the sun itself was embarrassed- yellow suit. I am not making this up, and from the quizzical looks this bloke was getting I wasn't the only one who thought he resembled a giant canary. Mind you, he was big enough to give King Kong a run for his money, so I wasn't going to inquire about his quirky taste in fashion.

One of the fun things about looking at the dress sense (an oxymoron here in the Land of Smiles) of other people is you can make a game of trying to determine from what part of this wonderful and exiguous planet they may emanate.

Although it is rare to see Germans, especially Bavarians, and Austrians strolling around in lederhosen it may only be because this kind of leather gear is a little too hot (in the sweaty armpit sense of the word) to be dragged out and dusted off in the Thai climate.

The 1970s may have been known as the decade style forgot, but I'm here to tell you flared pants and jeans, alligator-sole shoes and safari suits are alive and flourishing on many of the foreign tourists here in Bangkok and Pattaya. The only reason body shirts with the wide lapel collars aren't in vogue is most failed to make it past the 500th wash.

***

Equally, there are many men who don't want a permanent relationship, just sex without entanglements, so they come to Pattaya every year or every six months for two, three or four weeks and play the field as much as possible. These are the men Western women claim are afraid of the big 'C' word: commitment. More correctly, most are sick and tired of having to live up to some Hollywood-driven New Age idyll of the perfect man: tall, handsome, athletic, well-spoken, well-mannered, highly-educated and, most importantly, rich with a 'cool' job.

A large number of foreigners stay in some of the cheapest 'digs' they can find; eat only once or twice a day at the cheapest Thai eateries; drink in the cheapest bars, or sit outside their hotel with a bottle of Mekhong (a potent Thai whisky) and Coca-Cola or soda and try to avoid paying for sex with girls. They will wait until they find a girl they can get for free. Sometimes they splash out and take a girl from a beer bar, pay her 500 baht for the night and hope she will continue to go with them for nothing. By doing this they can extend their stay in the Land of the Lotus Eaters almost indefinitely.

Plenty of older men, retired from the workforce in their home countries, have taken up residence in Pattaya. Indeed Pattaya is becoming more and more like an old people's retirement village every year. In coming decades the place may have to be renamed 'Happy Acres' or 'God's Tropical Waiting Room'.

One 76-year-old Englishman told me he could live in relative luxury with his 31-year-old girlfriend instead of living a real hand-to-mouth existence in England. His English pension and the small amount of money he received on his investments were more than enough to keep him and his lady in fair style. The trade-off for the girl is she knows she will inherit most of his wealth when he finally turns up his toes.

Many of the expatriates in Pattaya tend to give the city a frontier-like edge. A large number are what could be termed 'fringe dwellers': freelance writers and artists, mercenaries, criminals and ex-criminals, standover men, drug dealers, renegades, and adventurers who enjoy a peripatetic lifestyle or cannot go back to their own country for whatever reason.

A large number of the resident expatriates technically stay in the country illegally. They have no work permit but run the go-go bars, beer bars, hotels, and restaurants and thereby keep the tourist economy bubbling along. The government is well aware of their existence and the vast amount of foreign exchange generated by these ex-pats. Only the real reprobates and those who have become a little too big for their boots incur the wrath of the Thai authorities and find themselves with a one-way ticket to elsewhere.

There are also a large number of 'steroid-heads' and 'gym-junkies', most of them from continental Europe, who spend plenty of time in Pattaya and are able to freely indulge in the taking of anabolic steroids, cheaply available over the counter at most of the various clinics (as the surrogate chemist shops are known).

As novelist Christopher Moore said in his interview with *The Big Chilli* magazine, "It is not the normal state of affairs for anyone to uproot a settled, or even unsettled, life and transplant themselves in a very difficult culture, learning a foreign language, and finding one's way cut off from childhood friends and family. That fact alone makes most of the people one meets highly unusual. Some are highly talented, some are badly damaged."

One interesting factor among expatriates is their general lack of knowledge of Thai, although linguistic experts agree the older a person the more difficult it is to learn a new language. A number of foreign men living in or visiting Thailand regularly speak little of the language, yet they demand their girlfriends speak at least passable English. A kind of language imperialism at work. The language is a mix of five tones and can be a minefield if you don't quite get it right. For example, an ex-pat Australian told me the story of his friend, who had learnt Thai from a book and when asked about the presence of snow in Australia said 'hee mah' (the genitalia of female dogs) instead of 'hee mah' (snow). This caused a not inconsiderable amount of merriment and giggling among the girls.

Other delights such as 'puke cow' (white skin), 'more fun' (believe it or not, this refers to the dentist), 'men' (feminists will love this one, it means 'bad smell') and the incredibly onomatopaeic 'chuck wow' (literally, fly a kite, but colloquially meaning male masturbation) provide plenty of listening pleasure.

The Thais are noted for their tolerance and understanding, and usually take kindly to anyone who attempts to learn even a little of the language. They may laugh at your rendition of the language, but they laugh with you, not at you.

***

One of the major downsides of the sex industry is the potential for sex workers to contract sexually transmitted diseases like herpes, syphilis, gonorrhea and other venereal infections. Since the early 1980s, the spread of HIV/AIDS has become a major health issue.

Unfortunately, reliable figures for Thailand are almost impossible to obtain and no matter where you turn, you find conflicting arguments, some claiming the country is in the grip of an epidemic while others allege it is no worse than many other nations.

The United Nations Development Program (UNDP) made a projection that by the year 2000 Thailand would have over 70,000 HIV-positive cases and 280,000 AIDS cases. An article in the 22 February 1993 edition of *Business Week* claimed around 600,000 Thais were already infected with HIV and up to 1,200 a day were expected to be added to the list. One book about the sex trade in Thailand, published in 1994, claimed the country might have over 5 million AIDS cases by the year 2000.

When I first visited Thailand, a friend who worked in the radio industry warned me saying, "67 percent of Thai prostitutes have AIDS." Where these figures came from I have no idea.

On another occasion, I was talking with two young English guys on their first visit to Thailand. One of them said, "I'm not going near the women; there was a BBC documentary on TV just before I left and it reckoned that 92 percent of Thai sex workers had AIDS." If either of the above figures were remotely true then Pattaya should now be a wasteland and AIDS should be rampant in Germany and England, two countries whose nationals frequent Pattaya on so-called sex tours.

The only way real figures can ever be obtained about the extent of HIV/AIDS in Pattaya is have the working girls tested on a regular basis by reliable medical practitioners. The cost of this form of testing for the average working girl is so prohibitive as to make it financially unviable. Therefore, many of the working girls, and boys, go largely untested for long periods of time, hardly an ideal situation.

However, a number of establishments have taken on the responsibility of trying to ensure their employees, at the very least, are as 'clean' as possible. The management of the Spicy Girls A Go-Go bar (formerly known as Papillon) made the decision to pay for a Government-appointed doctor to come in each week and conduct HIV tests on all their dancers. Interestingly, only one girl (who had been plying her trade from the bar for the previous two years) flatly refused to be tested. She was told to leave, while a few others also chose to leave the bar before undergoing testing. Of those who were tested, none showed up HIV-positive.

This photo, taken in 1971 and published in the *Bangkok World* newspaper, shows a Thai bargirl walking with an American tourist in a street in Bangkok. Where are they now?

Stereotyping Thailand

One evening in Sydney I spoke to an average young Australian, and his comments displayed the subtle depths to which the image of Thailand had sunk in the minds of those who blithely accept whatever they see on television, hear on radio, or read in print.

His first question was, "Is it true all Thai women are prostitutes?" a banal generalisation brought about by the stereotyping of an entire people by a media disinterested and unwilling to plumb the depths of reality.

People forget the sex industry in Australia-as it is, almost without exception, around the world- is a thriving part of the 'black' economy and a lot of money can be made by many of the women, and men, involved in it. Yet, few people mention Australia or England or the United States and prostitution in the same breath as readily as they do with Thailand.

In the most populous Australian state, New South Wales, it has been estimated between 20-30,000 women work full or part-time in the sex industry. This out of a State population of around 6 million. On a per capita basis, the numbers are not so different to those who work in the sex industry in Thailand.

The Eros Foundation, an organisation involved in working towards reform in the sex industry in Australia, stated within the Australian Capital Territory, a region based on Canberra, there were some 78,000 visits to brothels each year. The male population of Canberra numbers around 90,000 people and Eros claimed a significant portion of them visited brothels, even allowing for repeat attendances.

A 23-year-old woman studying for an arts degree at the Australian Catholic University admitted to working as a prostitute for some two and-a-half years while majoring in history. She claimed several students she knew also resorted to prostitution because they were unable to live on the study allowances given to them by the government.

Continuing to show his unintentional ignorance of Thailand, my young Australian friend also asked, "What about drugs. They hang you there don't they?"

This statement showed the blurring of lines between nationalities. I told him he was thinking about Malaysia, not Thailand. The Malaysians had hung two Australian drug traffickers in 1986 in an action that received widespread publicity and aroused condemnation in a number of countries. Thailand has not yet resorted to hanging foreign nationals for drug offences, although the prisons contain many sentenced to lengthy jail terms.

The 1997 economic slump in Thailand allegedly encouraged more people to become involved in the amphetamine trade. The secretary-general of the Office of Narcotics Control Board claimed Thailand was importing up to 80 million amphetamine tablets a year from jungle laboratories located in countries like Laos, Cambodia and Burma.

Because of the lower price of amphetamines (between 50-60 baht per tablet compared with 100 baht the year before) Thai authorities believed synthetic drugs had overtaken heroin as the drug of choice. Indeed, Thai narcotics police confiscated over 70 million amphetamine tablets in 2000.

In early 2003, Prime Minister Taksin Shinawatra launched what he termed a war on drugs designed to make the streets of Thailand drug-free by the end of April that year. In the weeks that followed the 'declaration of war' the price of illegal narcotics skyrocketed as literally hundreds of suspected drug addicts and dealers were gunned down. The police claimed most of the killings were high-level dealers 'silencing' the lower ranks, but many people suspected the close involvement of the men in brown. By the end of May, the total number of deaths related to the war on drugs numbered in the thousands, the vast majority unsolved.

During the 19th century, the Chinese controlled much of Thailand's drug trade. Triads dominated the Chinatown district of Bangkok and the Thai government, under the auspices of King Mongkut, actually allocated gambling, alcohol, lottery and opium monopolies to various secret society leaders. These monopolies accounted for nearly half the government's annual revenue. In an effort to prevent Thais becoming opium addicts, King Mongkut issued an edict compelling any Thai found guilty of smoking opium to wear a pigtail and pay the Chinese a tax. Consequently, very few Thais became opium addicts and the habit of smoking the drug did not take on. In June 1959, the government closed down the 900 previously licensed opium dens and banned the drug. Many of the dens were later turned into massage parlours.

Walking in downtown Pattaya or along the Beach Road promenade, it often happens that a voice whispers the magic words "marijuana" from the shadows. I have never been tempted to follow up the surreptitious offer. Lately, the equally magical words "cocaine" and "heroin" have also been whispered at me. I really will have to stop dressing like a society dropout.

There are many girls whose vices range from card playing and heavy drinking to drug taking; speed and 'ya ba' (crazy pill) being a favoured drug to keep a girl awake during the long hours of work. During the 2003 drug crackdown, many dancers seemed to gain rather a lot of weight. As the pressure eased off, these same dancers began once more to miraculously lose excess flab.

A former manager at one Pattaya hotel told me of his encounter with the police and drugs in Bangkok. He had not long made a purchase of marijuana from a Thai dealer when two Thai policemen confronted him. They searched him, found the marijuana and his immediate thought was, "oh, hell, 18-months to two years in a bloody Bangkok prison."

He continued, "They told me they were arresting me and we started to walk in what I supposed was the direction of the nearest police station. I was shit scared. However, we turned into a small alleyway and I thanked God because I knew they were going to shake me down for money. They asked me how much cash I had on me, but I only had about 2,000 baht. They said that wasn't enough so I told them I would go to a bank and could get them another 8,000 baht. They came with me while I got the money and then we went back to the alleyway. They took the money and the dope, but I was free to go."

Others have not been so fortunate. Bangkok's Khlong Prem prison is full of foreigners who thought they could fool the Thais and get away with drug smuggling.

***

Just how many people are negatively 'pump-primed' by their national media before they arrive in Thailand is hard to gauge. One night I was sitting with a girlfriend at her bar in *Soi* 2 when, at around 3:00 a.m., two foreign women and their boyfriends came to the bar. They turned out to be from Scotland and one of the women, who was well and truly drunk, decided of all the men perched on stools at the bar she would pick on me and, without introducing herself, said, "All you bloody men, you should all be ashamed of yourselves. What you do to these poor women, it's disgustin'. All men are absolute bastards. It's fuckin' cruel how they treat the women here. You don't treat an animal like this."

She was of average height and weight, with a shock of strawberry blonde hair, and rambled on with this vitriolic diatribe for a few more sentences. I then calmly asked her, "How long have you been in Pattaya?"

She replied, "We got here today."

"Oh," I said, "I suppose you'll be leaving this den of iniquity tomorrow then," adding a hint of sarcasm to my voice.

"No, we will not. We're goin' to be stayin' here for a few days," she replied in her broad Scottish brogue.

"Well, perhaps in a few days, after you've managed to speak to a few more of these 'downtrodden' souls you might obtain a clearer picture of the reality of this place," I stated.

She wandered off unappeased but came back later in the night, looked at me questioningly and asked, "I might have it wrong, eh?"

I told her many people on their first trip to Pattaya got the wrong impression of the international sex trade in the country. The foreign media painted pictures of women sold into virtual slavery and debt bondage or forced into prostitution by unscrupulous Thai and foreign males. This certainly did happen, not just in Thailand but in other countries as well, but with regard to the bars and the girls she was seeing in Pattaya nothing could be further from the truth.

From the first day a clutch of U.S. Marines managed to get lost and rattle into the little fishing village that was then Pattaya to the present when whole convoys of diesel-belching tour buses full of goggle-eyed north Asian vacationers clog the narrow streets of the international city, the world's media has generally looked down its collective noses.

Whole column inches of reportage appear pruriently engaged in fostering an image of a city awash with the kind of people who have given plastic raincoats a bad name. That your average garden-variety paedophile is attracted to Pattaya is not in question; only a fool would suggest otherwise. The vast majority of ex-pat residents and regular visitors to Fun City have nothing but contempt for those who would normally be found lurking outside primary schools in plastic raincoats and with a bag of lollies in their pockets.

"Have a good look at what's happening here tonight," I replied. "Look around at all these bands playing, look at the smiles and the laughter and the banter going on around you. How many sullen faces can you see? I'm not saying it's a bloody paradise but these girls are free to go or not to go with whomever they please."

Martin, a former partner in the Spicy Girls A Go-Go, told me of a conversation with a female producer from the BBC who was in Pattaya to do a story for British television. She told him that within 48 hours of being in the place she realised it was the men who were more likely to be exploited, not the women.

Around the same time, a 21-year-old girl I knew told me, "I have boyfriend England, France, and Italy. Actually I have three boyfriend England." All these men were sending her money so she didn't work the bars; one even bought her a house in her home province of Khorat. Nonetheless, she still went to her old place of employment and off with other men.

The foreign media's xenophobic 30-second television 'bites' and five-paragraph newspaper items describing the sex and drug industry in Thailand have effectively reduced the country to not much more than a den of iniquity inhabited by a mild and acquiescent people and preyed upon by a sub-human species of foreigner. Thailand...neatly pigeonholed and filed for future reference.

It’s amazing what the ingestion of enough alcohol will do to the average heterosexual male in Pattaya. ‘Elvis’ was the manager of the Giligin’s a-go-go in Pattayaland Soi 1. An American-owned chrome pole palace it closed its doors in 2003 after just over two years of operations. Married to a Thai lady, who bore him a son, ‘Elvis’ decided to take a walk on the wild side one evening. He probably should have barred people with cameras!

2

Only the Good Die Young

The Curse of the Motorbike

Pattaya is definitely not a quiet, tranquil beach resort. I am sure anybody who survived the Second World War in Europe must lay awake some nights and think the place is being dive-bombed by Stukas.

Motorbikes, ridden by foreigners and locals, scream down Second Road at all hours of the day and night, sounding like replicas of that feared German warplane. At a point along the Second Road, opposite the beer bars of *Soi* 9, there once stood a collection of motor vehicles that had failed to stop in time, and were now horribly mangled pieces of rusting metal. One can only imagine the fate of the occupants of such vehicles.

One of the most ambivalent aspects of life in Thailand is noise. For much of the outside world the view of Thailand is one of serenity, calm and smiling faces, at least in the rural areas and away from cities like Bangkok and Chiang Mai.

The reality is far different. Karaoke bars in villages that only got electricity about six months ago resonate to the sounds of people who definitely should never give up their day jobs.

Pattaya, for example, possesses the most incredible and amazing piece of musical devastation I've come across, in the form of the Hollywood Disco mobile ear-splitter and heart-pounder. This is a big, black-coloured utility with enough speakers mounted on its rear tray to make an Aerosmith concert look like a church organ recital conducted by Marcel Marceau.

The monster is launched upon an unsuspecting public and can be heard loud and clear long before it is ever seen. The threshold of pain on the Decibel Scale is 130, while a space rocket at take-off measures between 140 and 190 decibels. This vehicle without doubt rates close to the high level of a rocket taking off.

Had the former Iraqi dictator Saddam Hussein possessed this vehicle he would not have needed to invade Kuwait in 1990. All he had to do was park it at the border, turn it on and, after maybe two or three days at the most, every living thing, humans, animals, insects, amoeba, would have packed up and left town. Saddam could have marched into a vacant desert and just set up shop.

The Hollywood Disco is also one of the loudest places on the planet. Your heart starts pounding before you walk inside the joint. Once inside you can forget about any form of verbal communication. Even shouting your order directly into the ears of the waiters and waitresses is a wasted exercise. You stand at a circular Formica table and an ice bucket, a bottle of Thai whisky and a couple of bottles of mixers will be brought to you, along with enough glasses for the number of people with you. When it comes time to get the bill, you raise your left hand, palm outward, and with your right hand, you put your thumb and forefinger together and do a scribbling motion onto your left hand. What should eventually happen, is a flunky will appear at your table armed with a piece of paper on which is inscribed a number, usually large enough to significantly raise the GNP of several small Caribbean islands, and carrying a torch to illuminate said bill. And all the while, your brain is slowly but surely being evaporated by noise.

Although Pattaya may be able to lay claim to being the king of noise, the people of the country in general seem to love loud sound. From discos and karaoke bars to fruit vendors, campaigning politicians, and movie theatres who hire slow-moving utilities mounted with speakers to drive around the city blaring out the price of rambutan, election promises or the latest Thai film release, the average city and town is awash with noise.

This religious observance of sound is not a recent phenomenon. In January 1960 the *Bangkok Post* reported police had forbidden the use of loudspeakers advertising goods for sale and they instructed the public not to play radios loudly. As with most official pronouncements in the country, this one was universally ignored.

***

Southeast Asia is a motorbike manufacturer's paradise. The two-wheeled people movers clog the highways and byways of cities, towns and villages throughout Thailand and most other Asian nations.

Motorbikes come in all sizes and shapes. Most Thais ride the less powerful bikes (100cc and 150cc models) to go to and from work; go shopping, either singly or with the entire family aboard (husband, wife and two young children, and even a baby) and move house (including the furniture and the kitchen sink).

Bikes are relatively inexpensive to buy and cheap to rent and on my first trip to Pattaya I decided to take my life into my hands and hire a motorbike.

If the person who willingly signed out his precious motorbike to me had known my only previous biking experience involved a day of trail riding around a country property which culminated in me launching the said trail bike over a hillock, becoming briefly airborne before crashing to the ground and injuring my right knee I doubt he would have been filled with confidence. The accelerator had jammed while I was applying the brake, thus producing a catapulting affect. At least that's what I claimed at the time.

After a few 'kangaroo hops' down Beach Road (which no doubt amused the odd tourist and eagle-eyed Thai), I found myself feeling like Dennis Hopper in *Easy Rider* as I made my way towards Jomtien Beach, just over the hill from south Pattaya. To anyone else I probably looked more akin to Mr Bean.

Jomtien is the place where most sun lovers go to soak up the UV rays and swim. The water is cleaner, but only just, than in Pattaya Bay. The biggest danger in swimming at Jomtien was either being mown down by a lunatic on a jet ski or run over by a powerboat. The cacophony of sights and sounds is at times incredible. Apart from jet-skis and powerboats, hang-gliders and windsurfers abound in what is a playground full of water toys for grown-ups.

It's a European-style beach in that most sun-lovers take a seat in a deck chair shaded with a beach umbrella. A motley collection of people offering body massage, a manicure and pedicure, or selling sunglasses, wallets, Walkmans, food, and drink will suddenly descend like flies around guano.

At the time, it was possible to ride a motorbike without a helmet and so I was bedecked in sunglasses and a baseball cap. Going down the hill towards Jomtien the baseball cap flew off in the wind and I pulled over to the verge of the road, hopped off the bike and retrieved it. When I remounted the bike, I noticed a fair amount of traffic coming down the road. I 'gunned' the motor and took off into the road. Unfortunately, the verge consisted of loose gravel and my bike did a nice rear-wheel pirouette worthy of a Prima Ballerina before unceremoniously dumping me into the middle of the asphalt.

Thankfully, the approaching vehicles stopped to watch the embarrassing spectacle while I remounted the bike and continued onto the beach. At Jomtien, I checked the bike and found I had broken the right-hand mirror and scraped the right-hand side of the red duco. I was glad it was red because it masked the fact that not only was my pride damaged I had cut my knee and bled on the chassis.

I returned the bike later that day and was duly charged 500 baht for the damage. It was the first and last time I have ever hired a motorbike in Thailand- since then I have travelled on foot, by baht bus or motorbike taxi.

A few months later, I hired a motorbike while holidaying in northern Australia and proceeded to keep my perfect record of crashes intact. I managed to make a mess of my right knee and vowed I would never take control of the handlebars of a motorbike again. Forget all that garbage about falling off a horse and getting straight back on, motorbikes (at least those steered by me) and I have parted company forever.

Nevertheless, the 'curse of the motorbike' has continued to hound me. Early in 1999, I was in the process of crossing South Pattaya Road and after looking both ways and believing myself to be in the clear, I was suddenly upended by a Thai man who had scooted out of a side street. He and I became acutely acquainted with the road surface but, luckily, there were no serious injuries. Both my legs were cut and grazed while his machine and he remained in working condition. After offering humble apologies and mumbling concern over my welfare, he remounted his fallen steed and proceeded to 'putt-putt' off into the distance while I hobbled across to the other side of the street to lick my wounds.

***

Before I left Australia, I was warned about the dangers of picking up all sorts of vile gastro-intestinal diseases caused by eating food cooked by street vendors. As it happened, I managed to survive the street food and instead got a case of conjunctivitis (weepy eyes).

I am susceptible to eye problems of this nature and all that can be done is to bathe the offending eye- or in this case, eyes- in salty water and apply some drops. I went to one of the many clinics that serve as chemist shops and told them- as well as showed them- my problem. Even though my eyes were quite red and the 'sleep' in them was obvious, they gave me a bottle of eardrops.

Luckily, I noticed the label before applying the eardrops to my already bleary eyes. Perhaps they thought my eyes were too far gone and hoped to prevent the conjunctivitis spreading to my ears.

Mind you, this was not the worst thing to happen to me, in a medical sense, during my frequent visits to Thailand. Once, what started as a small sore on the back of my left calf gradually became worse over a period of a few days and grew in size to the point where I couldn't put my leg on the bed at night without discomfort.

Thinking what I had was not too serious I made my way to the Pattaya International Hospital to be checked. After filling out the usual forms, being weighed, prodded, and having my blood pressure taken, I was directed into a ward and asked to lie face down on a bed. I had an abscess and a male doctor's assistant decided to scrape it out without the benefit of a local anaesthetic. I sweated profusely as he dug out the blood and gore, wincing as he scraped away.

"Hurt, does it?" he inquired in Thai with a smile on his face.

"Yes, it hurts," I replied through clenched teeth.

"OK, I get anaesthetic."

He went and loaded a needle I'm sure was last used to subdue a rogue elephant and promptly skewered it into my calf. At least it worked and took away the pain.

After the wound was dressed, the head nurse told me to return every day to have the dressing changed and the wound cleaned.

"Alright, as long as you don't let the Marquis de Sade anywhere near me," I replied.

Second Bite of the Cherry

My second trip to Thailand was the first leg of a three-month holiday that included England and parts of Europe. Along with Mike and Janet, I once again spent most of my time in Pattaya and met a 19-year-old girl named Nan who worked out of the Sugar Shack Beer Bar, located across the road from the Anzac Hotel.

Nan was an impish character, full of life and very popular with the punters because of the ample size of her mammary glands. She was only average height and somewhat stocky but her bright personality and ready smile endeared her to everyone.

Nan came from Khorat and told me she had worked in a food hall in Bangkok before coming to Pattaya to work in the bars for the usual reason: lack of money to support her poor parents.

Nan and I became friends and I continued to see her until the following year when she told me she was getting a visa to go to Germany and marry her boyfriend. He was sending her 30,000 baht a month while she stayed in Thailand, a phenomenal sum for a young girl working in a beer bar.

About three years later, I ran into her cousin Oom in the Tahitian Queen A Go-Go and she told me Nan had been busy in the population stakes, producing two children.

With Mike, Janet and Nan, I went to a place called the Sida Resort, located outside Nakorn Nayok, northeast of Bangkok. We were picked up in Pattaya and taken to the resort by Janet's cousin, Jimmy.

Jimmy was an entrepreneur who specialised in supplying a range of goods to golf shops. He drove an expensive car, kept a couple of girlfriends and lived a lavish lifestyle.

Sida Resort was set in beautiful lush surroundings in mountainous countryside. A fast-flowing creek dissected the resort and in the mornings, a fine mist usually swathed the tops of the trees and lingered until mid-morning.

We stayed for three days, but when we to returned to Bangkok, we encountered heavy traffic coming up for a canoeing festival at a place called Sarika. The traffic was banked up for many kilometres and at one stage the entire road was blocked as the on-coming traffic endeavoured to create two and then three lanes out of one.

After dropping Mike and Janet off at a house in outer Bangkok, Jimmy drove Nan and I to the Fortune Hotel, in the Din Daeng area. Fortune was right, as a room cost 2,500 baht per night. It was close to Don Muang airport and my flight to Europe was the following afternoon.

It is recognised that newly industrialised countries at the 'gold taps' level of economic growth tend to focus on building gleaming new office blocks and residences while tearing down older buildings and neglecting their past. Bangkok and the main provincial capitals are classic examples of this rush to remove the past and embrace what is perceived as the future, and the Fortune Hotel was certainly in the vanguard. Indeed the contrasts could be gauged simply by looking out the window. From our room, Nan and I could look down to the rear of the hotel and see the rusty corrugated iron shacks that were home to probably hundreds of people who no doubt earned less in a month than I was paying for one night in the Fortune.

That 20 percent of the population earns just four percent of the wealth in the country may help explain why so many girls come to work in the sex trade in Pattaya and Bangkok.

Card Sharp

After spending a month in England and then moving through Europe before finishing up in the-then newly-opened up Czech capital of Prague, a beautiful city whose people I found surly and unsmiling (although there were notable exceptions) and who seemed determined to make any foreigner walk on the 'correct' side of any pathway, I returned to Thailand. I was happy to be heading to a country where I knew people would greet you with a smile and couldn't care less which side of the road you walked on. In fact, they didn't care on which side of the road you drove.

Even so, Thailand has gained a reputation for being a place where holidaymakers can be 'taken to the cleaners' in more ways than one. Scams involving fake or worthless gems, credit card fraud, shonky real estate deals, drugging on air-conditioned buses and dodgy card games are almost legendary, even though in reality most can only be successful with people who let greed get the better of their judgement.

Many Thais perceive foreigners as walking wallets. After all, the majority of Thais can't afford the price of a plane ticket to some exotic location like the French Riviera, let alone stay there and spend money. Therefore, Q.E.D., foreigners are extremely rich and if some of that wealth can be transferred, by fair means or foul, then so much the better.

I had been back in Pattaya for about a week and was out strolling in the busy southern part of town when an Asian man smiled at me and said, "Hello."

This fellow said his name was Al (I never found out, but maybe Capone was his surname) and he was half-Thai and half-Filipino. What a combination.

Taller than the average Thai and a little overweight, his English was excellent and he asked, "Where do you come from?"

"Australia," I replied.

"Oh," he perked up. "What city?"

"Sydney."

"Oh, my sister is going to Sydney to work as a nurse. Could you tell me if it is very expensive to rent rooms in Sydney and will it be safe for her?" he asked.

I offered to give him my address and said his sister could contact me when she arrived and I would introduce her to some Filipino and Thai people I knew.

He appeared happy with this and said, "Where are you going now?"

"Nowhere in particular, I was just out for a walk," I replied.

So my new best friend Al asked, "Would you like to come back to my place and meet my sister and my brother?"

I foolishly agreed to this seemingly innocent suggestion.

Al possessed a motorbike and I rode with him back to his house. It was a two-storey, white-walled, clean, terrace-style house a few minutes into the predominantly Thai area of south Pattaya. Inside, the furnishings looked a bit sparse: a laminated table for eating dinner, four chairs, a couple of lounge chairs and a glass-topped table. It had the air of a place that had been freshly rented.

Al introduced me to his brother Rowie, a smooth-talking, cigarette-smoking character with a conspiratorial voice who quickly assumed the role of chief conversationalist.

Rowie had the surreal aura of a gangster in a Mickey Spillane-style movie with a voice that sounded like a Mel Blanc cartoon character.

Rowie's wife, a surprisingly tall Filipino woman who looked in her mid-thirties, was introduced and then promptly made herself scarce.

Rowie maintained the "my sister's going to Sydney soon" story and apologised for the fact she wasn't at home. Rowie said she was having her hair done at the, "beauty parlour." I knew from that phrase he was more Filipino than Thai.

At any rate, Rowie and Al were very friendly and made me welcome with food and drink. At this stage, I certainly didn't feel like the fatted calf. After this bonhomie, Rowie told me what he did for a living.

"I am a card dealer in a casino located on a luxury cruise liner. The ship travels all around the region and I am only here for a couple of days until we sail again," Rowie stated.

He then asked if I played cards or was a gambling man. Is the Pope a Catholic?

"Ah, so what I have to tell you may be of some interest," said Rowie. "As a blackjack dealer I have a little side business going with my friends on board the ship."

I never did learn the cognomen of this fabled vessel. Probably the *Marie Celeste*.

"There are no security cameras on board the ship," he continued. "Just a few security guards. What we do takes no more than half an hour and I have the co-operation of the security guards and a couple of other people who work in the casino on the ship. We usually make about 10,000 American dollars each session but I only do it with foreigners I can trust. Out of that I pay my friends about 1,000 dollars each and give the foreigner 33 percent."

Rowie then asked if I'd be interested in finding out more about this little scam and, if I passed his test, to come on board the ship and play for real.

I agreed and said his brother would pick me up the next day, bring me back for lunch and Rowie would show me how the game was played. Al then took me back to the hotel on his motorbike.

The next day Al came to my hotel about 1:00 p.m. and took me back to the house. We had lunch and this time the 'sister' (remember her?) happened to be conveniently in Bangkok organising her visa for Australia. Rowie once again did all the talking and after the plates were cleared away pulled out a deck of cards.

He asked if I knew how to play blackjack.

"You have to get 21 and the dealer has to draw to 16 or 17 or something. Basically, the person with the highest total nearest 21 wins," I replied.

"If you knew which card was about to come out next, do you think you could win most of the time?" Rowie asked.

"I would think so."

"If you knew what cards your opponent was holding do you think you could win?"

"Absolutely."

"I am going to show you how we play on the ship and then we'll play a few practice rounds, for no money, to see if you have the hang of it. As you can imagine I need to know if you can play before I give you my money to play with on the ship," Rowie said.

Rowie then explained he gave his foreign accomplices the money with which to play on the "ship". He mentioned he had a number of friends from various countries who regularly participated in his little swindle.

Rowie then explained that on the "ship" the blackjack games he was involved in were usually two-person affairs. The intended victim would be coerced into being the banker and Rowie would sit alongside him and deal. The other person, his partner in crime so to speak, would sit opposite. Rowie would deal one card to the banker and one card to his accomplice. He would then surreptitiously reveal the next card to be dealt to the other player while peering at the card held by the banker. Then, by using a series of hand signals, he would indicate what that card happened to be.

Rowie then gave me a run-down of the hand signals.

"On the ship we never play for more than 20 or 30 minutes so as not to arouse suspicion."

So, while Rowie dealt, I played a few hands against his brother Al.

With the knowledge of my opponents' cards, courtesy of Rowie's hand signals, and knowing what was about to be dealt, I won easily.

Then came the crunch.

Rowie told me he had dealt for a private game the previous night at one of Pattaya's leading hotels. One of the players was a wealthy gold-dealer from Brunei who, Rowie claimed, won over U.S. $20,000 and given him a meagre $100 tip.

"It was a very poor tip from a man who had won so much money and I would like to take him down," he said.

Rowie said he had organised a re-match with the players at his house for later in the afternoon but had invited the Brunei businessman to come a little earlier.

"Do you think you could play against him and win?" he asked. He said the whole thing would only take half an hour at the most.

"When I ask you if you would like a cup of coffee or tea Mr Duncan,"-as Rowie called me- "That will be your signal to end the game. You will say no, you have some business to attend to and the next round will be the last."

After agreeing, we all went upstairs and set up a card table. After a few more practice sessions, the man from Brunei arrived.

"Mr Duncan," Rowie said. "This is Mr Mullah from Brunei."

Mr Mullah looked the part of a wealthy businessman. He wore a striped business shirt, had glasses, a potbelly, and gold rings on his fingers. I was dressed in a T-shirt and shorts and looked more like I spent my nights sheltering under beach umbrellas.

Rowie had earlier told me to inform Mr Mullah I had been playing banker all morning, had lost and would he mind playing the role for our session.

Mr Mullah grinned broadly, agreed to my request and sat next to Rowie.

Al sat next to me as Mr Mullah pulled out a huge wad of American notes. He handed this wad to Rowie who counted out $10,000. I thought to myself, 'I'm only carrying about 200 Aussie dollars, we'll have to play small until I win a few hands.'

I mentioned this to Mr Mullah and Rowie explained I had been cleaned out in my morning game but he would guarantee my credit. Mr Mullah seemed to accept this.

The first game was a small pot of a couple of hundred dollars that I won easily after remembering the hand signals Rowie had taught me. I also won the next couple of hands, and then drew one.

The pot slowly climbed as Mr Mullah kept upping the ante in an attempt to beat me. He kept losing and commented, "You're luck seems to have changed Mr Duncan."

I was beginning to fancy myself as a real card shark.

My 'winnings' had grown to over $10,000 when Rowie asked, "Mr Duncan, would you like a cup of tea or coffee?"

As planned, I declined and told Mr Mullah I had some business to attend to and this would have to be my last hand.

Rowie dealt two cards to each of us. Mine were a three and a two while according to Rowie's hand signals Mr Mullah was holding a 10 and a queen and was thus sitting on 20. The next card I knew in the deck was a six. I drew that card and the following one, which was a 10, giving me an unbeatable 21.

Mr Mullah, seeing me with four cards and knowing he was holding 20, upped the stakes quite a bit. Within seconds the pot had grown to $29,000.

Then came the sting.

"Mr Duncan. Before I show you my cards, I have to ask you. You have been very lucky betting on credit. How do I know, if I win this hand, that you can honour your commitment here?" said Mr Mullah.

Of course, I felt like telling him I had 21 and the worst thing that could happen would be a draw on this hand.

Instead, Rowie piped up and told Mr Mullah he could certainly guarantee my credit. He then asked Mr Mullah if he could step outside the room with me and discuss this in private. Mr Mullah agreed.

Outside, Rowie asked me what I had. I told him 21 and he seemed pleased. I told him there was no way I could guarantee such a large amount of money. Rowie said he had some friends he could contact to bring some money over and cover the pot until we won. However, he asked me if I could possibly get my hands on some gold. "It doesn't really matter how much, say $2,000 worth. Just enough to impress Mr Mullah. There's $16,000 at stake here. And $8,000 of that will be yours."

That was the bait.

We returned to the room and Rowie informed Mr Mullah I was going to arrange for sufficient funds to be brought to the house to satisfy him. Rowie then suggested we meet back at his house in one hour. To prevent any cheating our cards were sealed in separate envelopes and crosses were placed on the back so they couldn't be steamed open and the contents changed without leaving some sign of tampering.

After Mr Mullah left, Rowie went downstairs to ostensibly ring his friends and arrange for some money to be sent to him. I remained with Al upstairs. After about 10 minutes, Rowie returned with a long face. He claimed he hadn't been able to get in contact with his friends and said if I accompanied Al to a gold shop and managed to get some jewellery then we could probably appease Mr Mullah.

At this stage, I had been so caught up with the adrenalin rush of the moment I hadn't really considered the reality of the situation.

I jumped on the back of Al's bike and off we went to south Pattaya. While on the bike I thought to myself, 'these guys are kidding. Here I am, dressed as if I didn't have two-bob to rub together and I'm supposed to have convinced some gold-dealer from Brunei I'm a wealthy Australian having a bad run at blackjack.'

We had been playing for about half an hour and there hadn't been any sign of the other "players" who were supposed to be "coming later." I decided, in spite of the possibility of picking up eight big ones, I'd play it safe and not obtain any gold for Al and Rowie's use.

We went to one gold shop and I produced my Visa card. I knew the card had very little credit left and it would be highly unlikely I'd get the amount of gold Al thought necessary to satisfy Mr Mullah. Sure enough, the shop attendant came back and apologetically told me the card seemed to lack sufficient funds. I breathed a sigh of relief.

Al then suggested I go to the bank, obtain some cash and go back to the gold shop. Once again, I contrived to obtain insufficient cash for the purposes of buying gold. Al admitted defeat and we returned to his house.

By now it was well after 3:00 p.m. and the other "players" still had mysteriously not arrived.

When Al and I returned Rowie was waiting at the front door. He gave Al a suspicious wink and a nod.

Mr Mullah had already returned (that is if he ever left) and Rowie took me aside and asked me if I'd managed to obtain any gold. I told him I hadn't. He looked perturbed and claimed he had'nt any luck in obtaining funds from his so-called associates.

We went back upstairs and Rowie informed Mr Mullah I had been unable to obtain any guarantees. Mr Mullah looked unimpressed but accepted the situation and left.

"It does not matter, Mr Duncan, you and I will still be friends," Rowie said.

He told Al to take me back to my hotel and said he would come around the following night at 7:00 p.m. and introduce me to some female friends.

I never saw Rowie again.

So, what should have happened?

Based on the experience of other victims I would have returned with a decent amount of gold as surety. The un-tampered envelopes would have been opened and the game completed. Since I had 21, I would have won.

Mr Mullah would have insisted we play "just a couple more hands" to give him a chance. Suddenly the signals would have been incorrect and I would start losing. After a couple of hands, I would have been forced into using the gold I had obtained. Of course, I would lose that as well. I could then hardly start complaining about losing a rigged game.

As it was, the exercise in cultivating me as a 'mug' backfired on Rowie and Al.

The sister? I doubt she ever existed.

I did see Al a couple of weeks later. He was engaging another foreigner in conversation as I passed by. He didn't recognise me and I ignored him. I saw his intended victim a little while later. He had obviously not fallen for Al's special line of patter.

On another occasion, I was at my usual breakfast hangout on the Second Road sharing a table with Dave, a mate from Manchester. He told me a story about meeting this English guy the previous day who had asked him if he was interested in making a lot of money very easily. Dave asked me if I would go with him to check this guy out.

After finishing breakfast, we went around the corner into Pattaya Central Road and into the lobby of one of the mid-range hotels and asked for his contact.

A few minutes later, a very dodgy looking character named Chris came down. He was slightly less than average height with brown wavy hair and a wide face and he spoke with a cockney accent that could have come straight off the set of *Minder* or *The Bill.*

Chris claimed to have worked out a scam, "Wiv some gangsters in England, a very nasty lot let me tell you." I thought he was laying it on a bit thick.

A Barclays Bank manager, who happened to be nearing retirement age, was allegedly planning to give himself a nice little nest egg by siphoning off money from the accounts of millionaires living overseas.

"Now these millionaires only get their bank statements every ffree to six munfs, so they won't notice anyfin' missin' for some time," Chris said.

The money would go via a letter of credit into Manchester Dave's bank account in Pattaya. Dave would then withdraw 75 percent of the money and send it by letter of credit to another account in another country.

Dave would keep the remaining 25 percent as his commission. Chris claimed the initial amount would be £100,000 (about 6 million baht), followed by two more amounts of £250,000 (approx. 15 million baht). Therefore, Dave could make £150,000 just for the use of his bank account. It sounded like the classic scam artist's clincher line: tantalise the intended victim with phenomenal sums and appeal to their latent greed. Dave gave Chris his account number but the rub came at the end of the conversation.

Chris asked Dave if he could borrow 1,000 baht because, "I'm a bit short of the readies and I've got to go back to Bangkok tonight to see the bloke who's puttin' all this togevver. But I'll be back 'ere in a couple of days and I'll ring you if this fing's goin' ahead."

I told Dave I didn't really know what the little grub could do with his bank account number but suggested he go immediately to the bank and withdraw all but a couple of hundred baht, to keep the account open.

"That way if they manage to get access to your account there won't be much they can pilfer. Just go and open another account with a different bank and put your money in there," I told him.

"Did you see that? The little bugger got 1,000 baht out of me. If all this is bullshit and he was only trying to scam 1,000 baht out of me I'll bloody kill him," Dave said.

"He thinks I'm goin' home to England in a few days, but I've decided to stay a bit longer and if he comes back here and doesn't pay me back I'll bloody get him."

Needless to say, Chris never rang Dave and we never saw the "little bugger" again.

***

The most common form of scam in Thailand, especially in Bangkok involves gems and other precious stones. Foreigners are usually approached on the street by a friendly Thai who suggests they can purchase precious stones for a fraction of the normal price. They are taken to a factory where the hard sell is used and the hapless foreigner makes a purchase. Of course, the stones are about as valuable as a three-dollar note and would be best used as ornaments in a goldfish bowl.

Some legitimate places obtain their customers via the numerous tuk-tuk drivers of Bangkok. The tuk-tuk drivers will hang around Soi Cowboy, Nana Plaza, Patpong, Khao San Road, and anywhere else they think they might encounter tourists and offer them a discounted 'sightseeing' tour of the city.

I was taking a walk around the city when a tuk-tuk driver with good English pulled alongside the kerb and said, "I take you to look around Bangkok for one-hour, only 80 baht OK?"

I showed him my map and told him I wanted to look at a couple of places in particular.

"OK, I take you there, no problem."

However, once we were under way he said, "I take you to fashion place. They make the clothes, very good quality, not expensive, you can look, you not have to buy."

I told him I wasn't interested in purchasing anything at all, I just wanted to be given a ride to the sights I had asked about.

"OK, no problem, but if you can do this for me I can get a voucher for two litre of oil. You stay 10 minute and they give me for two litre. You help me and then I take you."

I thought, 'oh well, I may as well find out what the deal is for the poor hapless tourists who get caught up in this.'

Our first stop was the ubiquitous Indian tailor shop, somewhere along Sukhumvit Road.

"Good afternoon sir, would you be liking some suit, or shirt?" said the bespectacled 30-something gentleman as I strolled through the door.

"Can you show me a good example of your product?" I asked. He handed me a jacket and while I pretended to be checking the lining, cuffs and workmanship of his product he continued with his spiel.

“Where are you from?” continued the Indian, sounding more and more like a go-go bargirl.

“Australia.”

“Oh, I have many customer from Australia.”

“I’m sure you do.”

“I can do you a nice suit for 200 Australian dollars.”

“I’m sure you could.”

I did my best at a delaying action for a few minutes so the tuk-tuk man would get his two-litre voucher. He explained if I actually bought something then he would receive five litres. I told him not to get his hopes up.

“Would you like a few shirts? Only 40 dollars Australian.”

“No, thanks. I’m right for shirts and suits. Actually, I’m leaving tomorrow.”

“Oh, that would be no problem. I could make you a suit before you go.”

He had an answer for everything.

“I’m sure you could. I have a friend who buys his suits in Thailand but the man he deals with is unreliable. Perhaps I could take your card and...”

“Well why don’t I make a suit for you so you can show your friend the quality of my product?”

“I’m sure it is good,” I replied.

“You keep saying ‘you’re sure’, but maybe I’m just a good talker.”

“Maybe you are. But I’m not interested in taking anything.”

I felt I had played my part in the tuk-tuk bargain and made my escape.

The tuk-tuk driver told me he had received a voucher for two litres of petrol and then said he could get another two litres if I spent 10 minutes or so in a gem centre. I agreed to go along but he stressed the importance of not speaking any Thai once I went inside these places.

"Otherwise they know you have been here before and they will think I cheat them," he said.

I felt like saying "you are cheating them" but merely nodded in agreement.

After the gem dealer we went to yet another tailor and finally to a gem and souvenir dealer. We were greeted with great bonhomie at the door by a short, loud-voiced Hollywood-type character who put me in mind of a B-grade gangster, "Welcome, come in, welcome, sir."

A soft drink was thrust into my hands and I slowly made the rounds of the gem cabinets, feigning interest in one or two items. The rings varied in price, the minimum being around the 12,000 baht mark.

Once again I stretched the tour for long enough and the tuk-tuk driver was well pleased with his two litre petrol voucher. I had worked hard to provide him with a total of six litres of petrol vouchers.

The tuk-tuk driver, the vouchers safely ensconced in his pockets, suddenly became reluctant to travel too far and only briefly pulled up outside Chitralada Palace (the King's residence) before dropping me a good five minute walk from the Erawan shrine. He still wanted to be paid his 80 baht; I gave him 40 baht and walked off.

Lightning Jack's *not* Crocodile Dundee

One afternoon I went with Nan and some of the people who worked at the Sugar Shack Beer Bar to Koh Larn Island in Pattaya Bay. It takes about 15 minutes to reach by fast boat, and is a favourite playground for day-trippers.

On Koh Larn, I met an Australian from Melbourne who suggested I go to the relatively new Cheerleaders A Go-Go in south Pattaya, run by a fellow Australian.

I took him up on the invitation and that night wandered down to Cheerleaders. The owner was, as I wrote in my diary at the time, 'a fat guy named Peter... Came to Thailand five years ago. He claimed to be pulling 5,000 baht a day out of this bar and was opening a new one in the same street as the Anzac and is looking to sell a 13 percent stake in it.'

Since I was keen on remaining in the country- as long as I could find a way of making a living and not being bored out of my skull by not working- I decided to investigate the potential for getting involved in a new go-go bar.

One person I asked told me Peter was the type who sold 10 percent shares in bars to 20 different people. When I broached the subject with Peter that night, he rebutted the suggestion.

"You bring anybody you like in here to face me. I don't care who it is, you won't find anyone to support that crap." He sounded quite convincing and, like so many before me and so many after me, I was silly enough to want to turn a blind eye, as I didn't want to miss out on a share in what I thought would be a good bar. The conman gave me the only answer he could possibly give in the most strident manner possible. I therefore decided to get involved with

Peter's new venture and took a 10 percent stake in the future Lightning Jack's.

Although I wanted to stay in Thailand, I was wary and only willing to get my 'feet wet' as it were. I knew absolutely nothing about the bar business and figured this would be a good way to see if I liked it and if it would work.

My financial stake was not particularly high and therefore the return on my investment was not likely to be good enough to allow me to stay permanently in Pattaya. However, I was not as concerned about that as being sure of what I was doing. Had I known what the future would be, it would have been foolish to put one baht into the venture, although the wealth of stories, insights, and incidents to come out of the bar, as well as the number of friends I have made, probably made the venture a positive rather than a negative experience in the end. As it was, I joined the incredibly long list of foreigners who have come to Pattaya and invested money in a bar.

***

When some people first experience the bar scene they are apt to get a feeling, just as I did, that this might be the way of staying in the country on a more permanent basis. Buy a bar, be it a beer bar or a go-go, and relax as they watch their money make more money. Or so they think.

It looks so easy. Charge around 60-90 baht for a bottle of beer costing around 30-35 baht wholesale and, as long as there are enough customers, then it must be possible to live a nice, comfortable life in the Land of Smiles.

The problem is you first have to find a suitable place to purchase. Most foreigners usually buy a bar which is already up and running. For a watering hole that is reasonably successful, a three-year lease with a three-year option might cost upwards of 2 million baht to purchase.

The price will include 'key money' and this has to be paid again at the renewal of the lease in three years. Of course, the building housing the bar has a Thai landlord who can see what kind of trade is being conducted. But he, or she, won't care how things are going in three years when the key money is up for payment again.

Since the early 1990s, the AIDS scare, critically biased media coverage of Pattaya, and uncontrolled construction of new bars has seen the numbers of tourists level off to the extent there are now more bars than people to drink at them.

In the new millennium the terrorist attack against the World Trade Center on 11 September 2001, followed in 2002 by the Bali bombing, in 2003 by SARS, the second Gulf War and threats of continuing terrorist action in the world's resorts also served to damage tourism to Pattaya.

Although there are literally hundreds of thousands of individuals, both male and female (and some indeterminate), coming to Pattaya each year, the amount of places offering entertainment also number in the hundreds. So the average place should really only expect to cater to a regular clientele of- judging by current statistics- two Russians and a Chechen refugee in December and January, an Englishman and a rarely sober Scotsman from February until late March, a gaggle of lost Japanese for an hour or two in April, five US Marines in May and June, an out-of-work Australian in July and a German backpacker couple with hairy armpits in late September. For most of the rest of the time, the bar is more likely to be visited by stray mongrels looking for the odd scrap of food dropped by the half-dozen or so bored bar girls.

For the landlord, his or her only concern is that the owner renews the lease, pays the key money and is on time each month with the rent. Falling profits and smaller attendances mean little to the average landlord who will simply say if you don't wish to renew the lease then someone else will doubtless take the bar. In most cases, they're right. There always seems to be a never-ending supply of foreigners wanting to get into the bar scene.

The new owner has to transfer the trading licences into the name of a Thai person, usually his wife or a friend. A foreigner cannot legally own and run a bar, although he can form a company to operate it. Another problem is there are as many as 20 different licences to be obtained, or transferred, and all of them technically have to be available on the premises. The most important licences have to be displayed above the bar. The previous owner would almost certainly not have managed to obtain all the necessary licences and so the ones that may be missing will have to be applied for...in triplicate.

Once the forms for the varying licences have been filled out and submitted- with the required fee- it may take a seeming eternity for them to be officially signed and stamped by the appropriate authorities. The delays can be interminable and as the new owner is paying rent from the very start it is imperative he open for business.

Needless to say, the local police arrive on the doorstep and of course ask where the appropriate licences are to be found. There is an easy way around this problem. Tea money. A nice little amount handed to the local and the tourist police will be more than enough to keep them off your back...at least for a while.

In reality, the majority of bars in Pattaya operate illegally. Very few obtain all the requisite licences. In fact, without the aid of an influential local Thai businessman, politician or policeman the chances of ever getting all the licences are almost negligible.

Once most of the licences are obtained then an owner can rest a little easier. Most licences do not have expiry dates although this will not necessarily stop the local authorities landing on the doorstep and claiming a particular licence needs to be upgraded.

The actual running of the bar is hardly a smooth operation. Rent, electricity, water, and wages to pay once a month; making sure the ice box is stocked with both ice and booze, the spirits are plentiful and the coolers have plenty of beer for the multitude of customers who will hopefully come streaming through the doors.

Running a go-go bar can be marginally more profitable than a beer bar (as a general rule) but it is also much more difficult and expensive. Getting- and keeping- enough pretty or just plain attractive girls to entice customers through the door is an ongoing problem.

A competent mamasan- usually a retired working girl- has to be found. She has to be able to speak and read reasonable English and be good but firm with the girls. The mamasan then has to make sure the working girls are all 18 years of age or older, all have ID cards, are not doing drugs while at work and have had their weekly Sexually Transmitted Disease (STD) check and a three-monthly HIV/AIDS test. In some places girls carry a small booklet that will fit into most wallets or purses and must be presented at the bar each week with a recent date stamp and proof a clinic has found her to be without any nasty social diseases. Of course, whether the girl has had a genuine check-up or merely paid a few baht under the counter to get a 'clear' stamp is contentious.

***

So, with all these factors to consider I returned to Pattaya to begin the task of learning about, and running, a go-go bar with Peter Harrison.

Peter named the bar Lightning Jack's after the failed box office film made by Paul Hogan, the laconic Australian comic whose first film, *Crocodile Dundee*, had been such a huge hit. The name also proved, in the long run, to be a failure for a go-go bar.

Some of the dancers who plied their trade from the confines of Lightning Jack's.

The rent in Lightning Jack's was a high 30,000 baht per month. Electricity ran between 8-9,000 baht a month while water cost a mere 500 baht. We paid our mamasan a hefty 10,000 baht a month, and the dancers received 5,000 baht a month each (for about 12-14 girls). The DJ and cashier received 4,000 baht a month each; the four waitresses picked up 2,000 baht and a bar boy 1,500 baht. The cashier, waitresses, and the bar boy shared the tips each night.

Peter claimed he had to pay the tourist police 15,000 baht and the local police 15,000 baht a month as 'protection' money. Practically every other bar in Pattaya was apparently doing the same, although for varying amounts. I know we were paying some money to the police but given Peter's lavish lifestyle, I suspect it was not such an exorbitant sum. It was just a good unverifiable amount he could pocket each month instead of divvying up the spoils in a proper fashion.

So, before we even sold a beer we had monthly expenses amounting to something close to 170,000 baht.

Then you had to actually have some booze to sell and so we'd have bottles of vodka, bourbon, scotch, and copious amounts of Singha, Kloster, Amarit, and Carlsberg beers. In 1995, Heineken, Tiger, and Chang were unheard of.

We later installed Carlsberg draught beer (fresh from the keg) and go through a keg every couple of nights. Not that we sold much of it mind you. Peter was a tall man with an enormous girth and a thirst to match. Unfortunately his thirst was confined to copious quantities of Carlsberg draught rather than water.

Carlsberg Draught, a Danish beer, made a great impact on the drinking market when it was introduced, especially in the bars. When ordering it at some waterholes many service girls couldn't quite understand what was being requested. Punters would ask quite clearly for a "Carlsberg Draught", only to be met by blank stares.

One ex-pat said to me, "Nothing in the world sounds like Carlsberg Draught, yet they don't understand." He'd figured a way around this problem: "I ask for a Daft Karsberg. They understand me and never get the order wrong."

From the very first, we were up against the odds. You don't have to be a mathematical genius to work out we needed to sell at least 6,000 baht a night worth of booze (and the return from bar fines- but more about that later) to stay afloat. Considering we were selling beer at about 70 baht a bottle it meant we had to flog off about 87 drinks a night just to break even. That may not sound like a lot, and for some bars down on Walking Street, it certainly isn't. However, when you know most punters only stay for one or two drinks it is not hard to see you need 40-50 people through the bar every night of the week, 52 weeks of the year to have any chance of survival.

Lightning Jack's could fit around 30 people, although 20 was a more comfortable number. Given our location and the competition in the town, we were lucky if we ever had more than eight or 10 people in the bar at any one time.

Friday nights we conducted a Quiz that became very popular and we managed to attract upwards of 20 people for a couple of hours. Saturdays were also popular but from Sunday through to Thursday, there were times when you could fire a cannon through the front door and only hit a bored dancer.

Many of the go-go girls tend to run in packs of two, three or more. It is rare for just one girl to come to a go-go bar by herself and ask for work. Usually two, three, and sometimes four girls might arrive on the doorstep and approach the mamasan for work as dancers. If they happened to be stunners then of course they would be hired on the spot, but woe betide any bar that failed to bring in sufficient customers. Those same girls would be gone faster than whispers on the wind if they felt they could do better in another bar.

A girl I knew named Sorn initially worked in Classroom 2 and over the next few years, I saw her in Baby, Happy, Champion, Vixens, Spicy Girls, and World Wide A Go-Go's. She never stayed in any one bar long enough to accrue long service.

If they decide to stay in the bar, the girls may bring in even more of their friends to work as dancers. This may sound like a good idea but it isn't. If the owner of the bar has a problem with one of the girls and she decides to leave, the chances are most of her 'gang' will follow suit. A go-go bar without go-go dancers is a pretty sorry sight. The dancers are issued with numbers and one bar owner I know uses Bingo slang for some of his girls: 11 is legs, and given to a dancer with good pins while 88 (two fat ladies) is issued to a dancer whose former occupation may well have been that of Sumo champion of Udon Thani.

It is important a bar owner recognise the different groups within his bar. As in any social situation, conflicts and misunderstandings will arise, and this is where a good mamasan comes in handy.

The girls were free to go with whomever they liked. If they didn't care for a particular customer we would never compel them to go. I remember one girl who had been bar-fined by an English guy and the following night he came back to the bar and asked the girl if she'd like to go with him to Chiang Mai for a few days. She said no and he asked me to intervene on his behalf. I told him I would ask her but she was free to do whatever she liked.

"Why don't you want to go with him?" I asked. "He's offered you 500 baht a day plus food and expenses and a trip away from work for a few days."

"I don't like him," she replied matter-of-factly.

She claimed he hadn't been the type of man she thought he was going to be and so, despite the opportunity of a trip away, time off work, and easy money, she refused.

I told the Englishman, "She doesn't want to go, I'm sorry."

"Can't you make her?" he asked. "How stupid can she be? She'll get money and a trip and there's no guarantee if she stays working she'll get the same money over the next few days."

"I can't make her go if she doesn't want to. It really is up to her."

I couldn't quite fathom why some man would want to coerce a girl into spending all her time with him when she clearly didn't like him.

A customer would pay the bar fine, which in Lightning Jack's was 500 baht, and the girl would leave the bar. Of the 500 baht, she received 100 baht. Anything the customer paid was hers and hers alone.

Most go-go bars insist their girls have from four to 10 or more "offs", as the bar fines are called, each month. They also try to get their girls to have 30 or more lady drinks bought for them. In Lightning Jack's we didn't insist on either the bar fines or the drinks, but if a girl was conspicuously down then we would have a word with her.

The "offs" and the lady drinks would pay for a girl's salary. If a girl were bar-fined four times in the month then we would earn 1,600 baht. If she got her 30 drinks, we would make another 1,500 baht. That's a total of just over 3,000 baht. The girl would be paid a salary of 5,000 baht, so on a girl who just made the minimum we would actually be losing nearly 2,000 baht a month. However, because she had been bar-fined and obtained her required drinks it would mean she had attracted customers who would almost certainly have spent a reasonable amount of money in the bar.

In practice, many girls would never receive the full 5,000 baht salary. They were allowed to take two paid days off per month and other days if they organised them in advance. They had to work Friday and Saturday nights, because these are the busiest, and if they didn't their salary was 'cut' by 500 baht. This may seem harsh but these were the nights when we made our money for the week and we needed to have every available girl. If we didn't make money then very soon there wouldn't be a bar and the girls would have to go looking for work elsewhere.

There were also 'cuts' for being late or being late to get up and dance when it was their turn, although these 'cuts' were usually around 10 or 20 baht.

What would happen is at some point most girls would run late two or three days during the month and, depending on how late they were, would have salary cuts of between 10 and 50 baht. Some girls would take a day off without telling anyone and be cut 500 baht. At the end of the month, many girls wound up receiving 3-4,000 baht instead of 5,000 baht.

For us to actually make money out of a girl she needed to get her 30 drinks and be bar-fined nine times in a month. The 'best' girls used to go out 15 to 20 times a month and would attract 50 or more drinks. The 'worst' girls would be lucky to get 20 drinks and be bar-fined two or three times.

In general, apart from the odd abusive foreigner, the worst thing about being a go-go girl would probably be boredom. Coming to the same bar for 28 or 29 days a month from 7:00 p.m. until 2:00 a.m.; listening to the same songs night after night for a month or so; talking to the same types of people as customers would be enough to bore anyone. Nonetheless, it was easier work than cleaning rooms for 12 hours a day in a hotel or serve food as a waitress in a restaurant for eight or more hours.

No wonder so many of the girls stay at a bar for three or four months and then find another bar to and work in, or alternatively go back to the village for a couple of weeks. Still, it is probably more exciting than working day after day in a department store for less money, running a food stall or shop-house or being a street sweeper. It's also why many girls will stay at a bar where their friends are working for less salary than a bar next door may be offering. *Sanuk* ('fun'; 'good time') is an important ingredient in the Thai working girls' makeup.

Sanuk is perhaps the one word that sums up much about the Thai character. This capacity for having fun and enjoying themselves is perhaps part of the reason why the sex trade in Pattaya is so popular with foreign men. There is none of the furtiveness and backdoor creeping you associate with the plastic raincoat brigade. It's all out in the open, tolerated if not totally accepted. The only people who are forced to sneak about are those who are attracted to under-age boys and girls. Thankfully, they represent a minority of the international visitors to Pattaya.

Up Periscope

When I returned to Pattaya, Peter asked me to go down and manage Cheerleaders A Go-Go, the bar in which I had first met him.

The following night a group of Australian submariners came into Cheerleaders and managed to liven the place up all by themselves. A few had been in the night before and one, Roger*, dragged two of his close friends into the bar. One, Harry*, was already well and truly inebriated. He jumped up on stage with the girls and then expressed a desire to get decked out in a Cheerleaders uniform.

I really can't fathom the male attraction for getting drunk and then wanting to get dressed up in women's clothing, especially if you are a member of the armed forces, but then I'm no psychologist.

The uniform consisted of a white top and a short red and white striped mini-skirt and Harry was a big boy. We hunted around and found one that almost managed to fit. The skirt reached around to cover about 90 percent of his ample girth while the top would not fit at all, hardly surprising considering he weighed at least 120 kilograms. The skirt also exposed more of his posterior than it did when worn by the girls. Thankfully, he was wearing black swimming trunks under the skirt.

In this state of more undress than dress, he staggered out of the bar and went up Walking Street to the Jan Bar (now the Roo Bar). He returned after a couple of hours, even worse for wear.

After closing the bar at 2:00 a.m., I wandered with Roger and Harry, still bedecked in his Cheerleaders finery, up Walking Street. I walked a few metres behind in order to watch the reaction of the girls, foreigners and lady-boys

The Australian submariner is a dainty creature. These boys added a new meaning to having a 'skirt in every port'.

(*katoeys*) as he wandered past. Needless to say, he received some interesting and bemused looks from the assembled patrons of various bars and eating establishments.

As we made it into Soi Diamond, he decided to race across the street into a series of bars and then inexplicably decided to remove his swimming trunks before rejoining us. A couple of Thai girls came over and lifted his skirt, exposed his less than tumescent member, giggled and ran off. He then decided to restore some of his dignity by putting his swimmers back on. Thank God.

I left Roger and Harry to their own devices around 4:00 a.m. and went upstairs in Soi Diamond to J. Fox Kitchen (then a Thai disco, now Big Willies A Go-Go) where I joined a couple of Lightning Jack's dancers for a drink.

The Australian media later went into yet another feeding frenzy almost four years after these submariners left our fair shores. A video, showing an incident involving the hazing of newcomers as they crossed the Equator for the first time aboard a submarine, came to light. The video showed the young sailors being forced into slime-filled garbage bins above decks before jumping into the ocean to cleanse themselves. One of those forced to submit to this hazing went public about the incident, which occurred to him in 1995 (the same trip that saw them come to Pattaya), in late 1998.

The general public was shocked and outraged and the usual calls for Royal Commissions, Naval Inquiries, Boards of Review, floggings, and walking of the plank went up. I found it funny and not really surprising that these were the same men who enjoyed themselves immensely while on shore leave in Pattaya.

* Not their real names

World Singha Beer Drinking Championship

Usually during the months of May and June, Thailand plays host to 'Cobra Gold', a series of war games the military hierarchy of the United States conducts every year with its closest ally in southeast Asia. The games involve a large number of US warships and Marine Corps troops pretending to invade, shoot, blow up and generally make mayhem in the name of defence.

Really, it's just an excuse for the big boys to go out and play with the expensive 'toys' their respective governments have purchased for them. It's also a good excuse for a massive booze fest.

In late May, Lightning Jack's conducted what we called the 'World Singha Beer Drinking Championship'. This was an impromptu event we ran to take advantage of the United States Marines then in Pattaya. We had become a major watering hole for the Marines, but not the ordinary US sailors, because we had gone out of our way to promote ourselves as a 'Marine' bar.

Early in the 'Cobra Gold' exercises Peter was in the bar one night when a Marine bemoaned the fact that all the bars in Pattaya seemed to have signs out the front welcoming the US Navy. The Marines, he lamented, had not rated a mention. Peter, being the smart marketing man (read conman) he was, immediately erected 'welcome US Marines' signs.

Word spread among the Marines and Lightning Jack's became their first 'port-of-call' on the way to a night of drinking and carousing. While other bars struggled, we did extremely well that month.

The patronage of the Marines contributed to a record one-night turnover figure at Lightning Jack's of nearly 31,000 baht.

A whole bunch of Marines used to come into Lightning Jack's as regulars, with Linda, our half-African-American, half-Thai mamasan, a major attraction. Linda was a second-generation sex worker. Her mother had been on the game during the 1970s and become pregnant to an African-American Vietnam veteran on R&R.

Linda was tall for a Thai girl, very dark with African features and a wild mane of frizzed hair. She was especially attracted, perhaps not surprisingly, to Americans and particularly African-American men. She was quite intelligent, being fluent in speaking, reading and writing English. She agreed to become Lightning Jacks' mamasan so she did not have to continue working in the bars. Of course, she still plied her trade as, and when she felt like it, but she was well paid as mamasan and could therefore be far more selective in her choice of clientele.

Later, Peter (in a typical fit of pique) sacked Linda as mamasan and brought back Noy, who had been the Cheerleaders mamasan. Linda went back 'on the game' and I saw her quite regularly over the next few years.

On one occasion, the US Marines ceremoniously presented us with a Marine Corps flag. According to the lieutenant in command, the flag had been placed aboard a US transport plane after the aircraft had been diverted to Okinawa. It had then been delivered specially to Pattaya so it could be presented to us. Of course, the Marine Corps commanders were blissfully unaware their esteemed symbol was to be hung in a Pattaya go-go bar.

The Yanks claimed they could drink copious quantities of alcohol without it having much effect. I was in the bar one night when a group of them started drinking Applecorn shooters. Applecorn is an apple-based liqueur that is downed in one mouthful. One of the Americans boldly proclaimed, “I can drink plenty of this stuff, man. It has no effect on me.” I saw him at about 2:00 a.m. practically unable to stand and certainly incapable of stringing more than two words together. I didn’t have the heart to ask him how he felt, as I’m sure later that day he was going to be nursing the mother of all hangovers.

One night Peter put it to them that they should get their number one drinker and match him against Som, one of our dancers who we claimed was the ‘World Singha Beer Drinking’ champion.

Som, nicknamed ‘Mr Ed’ because of a mouthful of teeth that went in every direction except straight, was 24 years old and had a five-year-old daughter. Som was from Khorat and had worked on building sites for three years before deciding being a bargirl was easier and definitely more lucrative. However, she kept making bad choices of Thai boyfriends.

Some Thai men just live off the earnings of their girlfriends. They hang out in Thai bars drinking whisky, playing snooker and pool, gambling, and usually finding other girls to entertain them while their girlfriend works in a go-go. They then demand all or most of their girlfriends’ money and hit them if they don’t comply. They are known as *meng da*, the Thai word for pimp.

Som found one of her beaus with another girl, but even after splitting with him he kept coming to the outside of Lightning Jack’s to see her. He was hoping to get back with her, not because he loved her but because she used to give him money and he didn’t have to go and work. I told her to forget him and look for someone better and different.

Som liked her beer and Peter claimed he’d seen her drink strong men under the table. In fact, Som won a previous ‘Singha Beer Drinking Championship’ in the old Cheerleaders A Go-Go, outpacing an Englishman.

Peter said Singha beer was unlike many other drops of the amber fluid in that it was hard to digest. Thais used to the texture of the beer (a cross between the sludge of the Chao Phrya River and a desalination plant), were generally capable of drinking large amounts, quickly, of the brew.

The Americans took the bait and we set up four tables with two 375ml bottles of Singha beer on each table.

Peter was determined to win and although he believed Som would triumph he decided to give her a 'helping' hand. Som's four bottles of Singha were nice and cold whereas of the four bottles the American was to drink, only three were cold. The third of the four bottles was warm. Peter figured once the American got through the third bottle he wouldn't be able to match it with Som. The participants were allowed to 'spill' up to half of each of the first three bottles, but had to consume the entire fourth bottle to win.

The American was named Sam. He was a young 22-year-old who clearly liked his beer and was going to do his best to keep the flag of the United States flying proudly and uphold the lofty traditions of the US Marine Corps.

He never stood a chance.

When the contest began, there were about eight Americans in the bar as well as around nine dancers and three service girls. With the girls screaming for Som and the Yanks yelling encouragement to their man, the contest began.

Som got away to a brilliant start by downing the first two very quickly, although she'd 'spilled' plenty of the amber fluid in the process. Sam began a bit slowly and was still on his second bottle when Som reached her third. She slowed considerably on the third bottle and coming to the fourth and final bottle, Som sat at the table and promptly slumped into her seat. It looked as though she had gone out too fast. However, she responded to the exhortations of her compatriots and raised herself for an attempt at the final bottle. Pushing herself to an upright position, she clasped it

As the beer flows freely (and not always down the throat), Som races away to an early lead.

to her lips. In the meantime, Sam, urged on by his comrades, also made it to the last bottle.

The battle was now well and truly joined.

The atmosphere in the bar was one of pandemonium as the two went slurp for slurp. As soon as the last drop had been drained from her bottle Som crumpled into her seat.

For Sam, the warm contents of the third bottle caught up with him as he downed the last of the amber fluid. He was unable to continue his charge home and Som managed to hang on and score a dramatic victory.

The girls were ecstatic and broke out in wild cheering.

Peter, taking full advantage of the occasion, held up Som's right arm as the winner of the 'bout'. Sam hung his head in shame.

The next day, the girls from the Billion Bar across the road asked me if we had been running an orgy the previous night. The noise had been so loud they thought we'd been running a full-on sex show.

Peter later confessed to rigging the competition to Sam and the other boys. They took it in very good humour and continued to come back to the bar until the end of the 'Cobra Gold' exercises.

Som continued to ply her trade, moving from bar to bar until, a couple of years later, she suffered a nasty motorbike accident. The left side of her jaw was broken and left a thin scar on her cheek. Her left leg had also been broken and made dancing impossible. She was reduced to working out the front of her bar as a barker, trying to entice customers into the go-go. She eventually healed sufficiently to go back and work as a dancer in Drop-In A Go-Go (now Folies Pigalle), the former Cheerleaders. Her new boyfriend was the DJ in Drop-In. Needless to say, she was still being bar-fined by foreigners.

Som, urged on by her dancing mates, raises herself up for one last attempt at ending the battle. Sam starts on his last bottle.

Kill the Messenger

Peter was a desperate gambler, usually using money he could ill-afford to lose or didn't have. One night after Lightning Jack's closed, I hopped on the back of his small motorbike (no mean feat considering Peter's enormous girth) and we went down Second Road to one of the misnamed Ocean View Bars at Soi 9.

We sat at a beer bar and got involved in a dice game with Fred, the German bar owner. The game involved the use of six dice with each player having three potential throws of the die. The first roll was a qualifying round in which a four, five and six must appear in order for the round to continue. After each roll, a minimum of one dice was removed. After three rounds (and assuming that a four, five and six have appeared at some point in those three rounds), there would be just three dice left. A final throw decided a player's final score and the highest total thrown won the round. To win overall, a player must win three games in a row. If, as I managed to do, you roll three sixes then you cannot be beaten and collect 1,000 baht.

Before we started to play, Peter handed me 2,000 baht and said, "We're in this together. If I win, I'll go halves with you; if you win, you go halves with me. OK?"

"Sure," I replied.

"I want to beat this German. He got me last night for a few thousand baht and I want to get it back."

We played for an hour or two but at the end of it, I had lost about 1,000 baht to the German and the German lost 1,000 baht to Peter. We ended up even.

***

The next night was Peter's 38th birthday. As is traditional in the bar scene in Pattaya a major party was conducted with balloons festooning the bar, a pig on a spit as the main fare, a birthday cake, plenty of free drinks, and shows. There are people living in Pattaya who virtually survive by chasing balloons and parties all over town. They are regulars at all the free food parties around Fun Town and despised by most expatriates.

The bar was packed almost from opening to closing. Late in the night, an army colonel turned up accompanied by a scraggy-looking longhaired guy who could have easily passed for a homeless derelict. The derelict said he wanted to kill John, our Thai landlord, because he claimed he had stolen the derelict's ideas for our bar. In order to prove his connections he asked me to come outside. I went with him around the corner into the next *soi* where went to the side of a green late-model Mercedes. Hanging inside the rear door was a colonel's uniform, complete with a row of 'fruit salad'. How the colonel, a staff officer at the Planning and Exercise Division in Bangkok, became involved with the murderous derelict I will never know. Maybe he was the colonel's wife's younger brother or something. The derelict asked if I would mind if he organised to have the landlord killed. Had I been just a little prescient, a simple "yes" would have saved me a few months of problems. Instead I told the derelict he should cool his heels for the time being as John was known to be well connected with the local mafia.

I relayed the story to Peter and after they left he said, "You're in charge of two departments- blowing up balloons and killing people."

I returned home to Australia a few days later with the intention of coming back to Thailand in a couple of months. Ah, the best laid plans of mice and men...

***

Peter had been in trouble with the Thai authorities on a previous occasion, telling me he once spent 70 days in jail in Phuket. He claimed he'd been told upon his release he was not allowed to overstay his visa in Thailand.

When I left, he was already overdue for his visa run but managed to enlist the help of a former employer, a fellow expatriate Australian, who used his connections to extend Peter's visa, but only for a few days.

The first I knew of impending trouble was just 12 days after I was back in Sydney. I received a message at the Rosehill horse races on the Saturday asking me to call Peter's father in Melbourne.

"Mate, Pete's in Kuala Lumpur and can't get back into Thailand," his father told me, "he's got no money and we haven't got anything either."

His father sounded completely disinterested in his son's plight and gave me the telephone number of the hotel where Peter was holed up. I rang him after the races.

"Duncan, I need you to go back to Pattaya as soon as possible. They won't let me back into Thailand. Mate, we'll have to sell the bar. But I need you to come here to Kuala Lumpur first and then go to Pattaya. I've got no money for food and can't pay the hotel bill and I daren't go out in case they ask me for some money. The next time I'll eat is when you get here," Peter told me.

First thing Monday morning I raced down to the local travel agent and booked a flight to Kuala Lumpur, with a connection to Bangkok for the day after. As the booking was hurried (I was given only two hours to get to the airport), I paid a premium of 1,400 Australian dollars for the Kuala Lumpur-Bangkok-Sydney flight. The Malaysian Airlines plane went via Melbourne and I landed in the Malaysian capital about nine hours later.

I rang Peter from the airport and he gave me the address and directions to his hotel in the Chinatown district. He looked very much the worse for wear. Peter suffered from severe gout and when we went outside to eat at a roadside restaurant, he took forever to move. He was unable to walk for any length of time or distance. The dinner I bought for him he said was the first food to pass his lips for four days.

He then explained what had happened.

"After you left I was overstay on my visa and when I went to Penang the consulate wouldn't renew it. So, I came down here and decided to get a new passport from the Australian embassy. I then took a flight from here to Bangkok without a visa. When I got to Bangkok they asked me if I'd ever been to Thailand before and when I said 'yes' they took me away to a private room and told me I couldn't enter the country. I should have bloody well said 'no' when they asked me if I'd been there before. It was a brand new passport so they might not have known. Anyway, they put me on a plane back to Kuala Lumpur and that's when I came to this hotel and tried to get hold of you."

The next morning I bought Peter a plane ticket for Manila in the Philippines, as well as going to the local chemist and buying some pills to ease his gout. I gave him a few hundred Australian dollars and he gave me the key to his condominium in Pattaya.

"The rent's due on it, but I think you should be able to stay there for a few days until you sort things out," he said.

Peter continued, "Don't talk to anyone. Don't tell anyone where I am; tell them I've gone home to Australia because my Dad's sick. Ray and Stan [the owners of Classroom A Go-Go] can't know what's happened otherwise they'll shut the bar before you can blink. And don't talk to Mike [a Pattaya real estate agent and erstwhile partner of Peter's in Cheerleaders A-Go-Go], he's not on our side either. We're on our own."

I flew from Kuala Lumpur to Bangkok in the early afternoon and took a taxi to Peter's condo at the Yensabai apartments in Pattaya. The task before me was somewhat daunting in that I was going to try to run and sell a go-go bar in low season without the majority shareholder present to oversee the operation.

I went down to Lightning Jack's, dropping in at the Anzac Hotel on the way to speak to Ron. He was an ex-Australian soldier who was managing the Anzac. Ron told me the bar had gone downhill rapidly after Peter left. The DJ started playing Thai music and, with Pattaya already in the low season, it quickly lost its few regulars.

I went to the bar and saw a place in chaos. The girls were coming in when they felt like it and dancing much the same. Noi, the mamasan, had been in contact with Peter who told her I was on my way and she was to give me the takings she had been keeping since he left. It didn't amount to much more than 24,000 baht, just enough to cover my airfare and the money I'd given Peter.

My presence, of course, put an end to the Thai music and soon the girls were dancing, albeit to an empty bar. A few customers drifted in and out during the night but not enough to make the future look anything but bleak, at least in the short-term.

Towards 2:00 a.m., when we normally closed the bar, Ron came up for a drink and a chat. Not long after he arrived, a very drunk Ray made his way into the bar. He started carrying on claiming Peter owed him money and his departure meant he, Ray, now "owned" Lightning Jack's. He also blamed Peter for the prospect of him "losing" his wife, although how Peter was responsible for Ray's marital problems was lost on me.

Ray, when drunk, was a belligerent character who liked nothing more than a good fight. He came over and, catching sight of Ron out of the corner of his eye, asked, "Is he your bodyguard?"

"No," I replied. "Why don't you go home and come back tomorrow when you're sober and we'll talk later."

Ron disliked Ray and a few seconds later they were eyeballing each other. The next second Ray swung the glass in his left hand at the side of Ron's face. The glass smashed and cut Ron's cheek. It was the last time he connected; Ron also liked a good fight and his military training meant he was quite proficient. Ron soon had Ray on the ground and gave him a good hiding.

The following night Ray's business partner Stan came into Lightning Jack's with the manager of his go-go bar in tow for protection.

"I hear you had a bit of trouble with Ray last night," he said.

Stan proceeded to threaten to close the bar at the end of the month if the bills he alleged were owed by my girls for clothes purchased at his Classroom Boutique were not paid. I told him I'd look into it and if the bills were due they would be paid out of the girls' salaries. I told him he was silly to let go-go girls buy anything on credit.

Within a few days, the bar started picking up and attracting a few more drinkers. However, doing a calculation of the amount of money I needed by the end of the month to pay rent, electricity and salaries and I knew we would be 80-100,000 baht short. I had arrived in the middle of the month and had just 16 days of trading to come up with the cash I needed.

In addition, Peter was ringing the Anzac Hotel and reversing the charges or asking me to ring him in the Philippines to apprise him of the on-going situation. These phone calls were not cheap and I ended up paying a bill of 9,000 baht to cover the costs.

It was imperative to sell the bar before the end of the month; either that or I might be compelled to do a runner with what I had and not worry about the girls and my reputation.

I spoke with Grecian (as in Grecian 2000, the hair dye) Ron- an Australian who owned a beer bar in the Best Friend complex- about leaving on the first available plane back to Sydney at the end of the month.

"No, don't do that. We'll find a way around the problem," he said.

"I don't want to do it, but I know I won't have the money I need to cover all the expenses," I said.

No one believed my story about Peter going home to Australia to see his sick father. Even John, the landlord, would ask me when Peter was coming back and after yet another evasive answer from me would say, "Peter not come back Thailand, I know for sure."

I decided I needed an ally and so, without Peter's knowledge, I went to see Mike, his former partner in Cheerleaders A Go-Go and gave him all the information he wanted. Peter had left Thailand owing Mike a lot of money and I thought it only fair he should know what was really going on. He offered to try to help in the sale of the bar, although he was also involved in trying to sell the old Cheerleaders A Go-Go, closed since the end of April.

What I perceived as my saviour came in an unusual form.

Each morning I would have breakfast, and then usually lunch, at a small cafe in Soi Skaw Beach, a side street just off Second Road. An Englishman named Charlie and his Thai wife Orr ran the cafe. She had lived in England for a time and could make bacon and eggs as well as anybody I ever knew; and her massaman curry was superb.

Charlie and I got on rather well and I told him I was looking to sell the bar. I said there were plenty of people making noises about getting the bar but no one had yet come up with cold, hard cash.

One morning Charlie told me the lease on his cafe and the rooms upstairs would soon be due and he would be looking around for another business. He expressed an interest in buying Lightning Jack's as long as I was willing to stay on with him and help run it.

Peter wanted to sell the bar for around 1 million baht but told me, "Don't be greedy, get whatever you can for it. We'll make a loss but we'll just have to wear it."

I said to Charlie I'd be prepared to sell the bar to him for 600,000 baht and he agreed. I rang Peter, told him and the deal was soon set up.

To show his good faith Charlie gave me the 80,000 baht I needed to cover the rent, electricity and wages at the end of the month.

Charlie and Peter spoke to each other on the phone one afternoon and agreed to the deal. Unfortunately, a couple of nights later the whole thing fell apart when John, the landlord, imposed himself on the negotiations. Charlie and Orr had come down to Lightning Jack's to sign the necessary papers when John dropped his bombshell.

"I not let you sell the bar," he told me.

"Why not?"

"Peter not own this bar. He not sign the lease before because he say he don't want to pay 2,000 baht to lawyer."

I had no way of knowing if that was true, although given Peter's general attitude, it probably was.

"I sell the bar to this man. I'm sorry, I know you lose money, but I sell the bar," John continued, looking anything but sorry.

I was snookered. My name did not appear on any legal documents with regard to the bar. I was in Thailand on a tourist visa, not a work permit, so I knew I couldn't approach the authorities. Without Peter around to make a fuss, I didn't have a clue what to do, so I was compelled to let John sell the bar directly to Charlie and Orr.

That night I received a phone call from Peter in the Philippines. On the verandah outside the front entrance to the bar was a red phone, the property of the karaoke bar next door.

“Duncan, what’s happened?” were his first words.

I explained Charlie had been willing to buy the bar for 600,000 baht but John had stepped in and said I couldn’t sell the bar because he (Peter) had failed to sign the original lease back in February. John said he was repossessing the bar and would sell it to Charlie, cutting both Peter and I out of the deal.

“Basically, we’ve done our money,” I concluded.

“No, you’ve got your money,” he said angrily. “And you’ve ripped me off. You’ve tried to dud a dudder, but I’ll tell you now you won’t get away with this. You and Charlie are off and you’re both off in a big way,” and then he slammed down the receiver.

This was the gratitude I received for having dropped everything in Australia, flown to Kuala Lumpur at some expense, paid his hotel bill, bought him food and pills for his gout, given him money, and purchased a plane ticket to Manila. No one else would have done what I had; but then Peter was the type who thought the world owed him a living.

Prior to my leaving for Australia a couple of weeks later, Peter rang the Anzac Hotel and asked Ron to come up to Lightning Jack’s, where I was trying to help Charlie, and bash me. Ron refused.

Three years later my neighbour in Sydney received a phone call at 3:30 a.m. one Sunday, the caller asking her to get me, as it was very important.

I picked up the receiver and the voice responded, “Duncan, it’s Peter Harrison here you filthy stinking piece of shit. You remember me do you? You arsehole, you thought I’d forgotten about you after three years didn’t you, you little shit, well I’ve tracked you down, I’ve got your phone number, the noose is tightening around you, you fucking dickhead...”

He went on in this vitriolic fashion, mouthing obscenities and barely pausing for breath as he made threats. He sounded like he might self-combust, and at the very least I could imagine his contorted features as he no doubt frothed at the mouth.

His unreasoned hatred of me had become an obsession; it may well have been the one thing keeping him alive, the desire to wreak some form of vengeance against me. It was ironic: I had been the one person he relied upon and because I failed to deliver what he deemed an appropriate outcome, he focused all his venom against me. As the messenger, I had been the bearer of bad news. Solution: kill the messenger.

***

Lightning Jack's struggled with Charlie at the helm and eventually closed down as a go-go bar. After a couple of ownership changes it eventually became known as Pussy Galore, a sports and beer bar, complete with a pool table and short-time girls. It was in this bar some of the *60 Minutes* footage (see 'The Ugly Australians') was shot and out of which two of the girls featured on the program worked. The irony was not lost on me.

***

Pattaya is much like a small country town. Rumours, no matter how fanciful, abound and reality takes a serious dive with people wanting to hear the latest 'gossip', be it truth or fantasy.

Mark, the former English part owner of the Anzac, said he was surprised to see me just a couple of months following the sale of Lightning Jack's to Charlie.

"We were told you were in jail in Australia," he said.

"Oh, who told you that?" I asked.

"[Grecian] Ron had apparently been speaking to Peter in the Philippines and he told him he had put you in to the authorities about drug smuggling and you'd been arrested and jailed."

I laughed and said, "Well, I only went home about eight weeks ago and I'm back here. If I was on bail or something I don't think I would have been let out of the country."

"Actually, I'm a bit embarrassed to say I accepted what I was told, even though I know this town is always full of bullshit. I even wrote to M [a former Anzac Hotel manager] in jail in Bangkok and spread the rumour," he admitted.

The whole thing sounded typical of the Walter Mitty element in Peter's character.

Ron, who had just bought out Mark and Tony to take over the Anzac, told me I should be careful, "there are death threats flying all over the place."

Later that day I went to visit Orr in hospital. She had been knocked off her motorbike three days before I arrived in Thailand and had undergone surgery. Instead of doing the usual thing and fleeing the scene, the driver of the offending vehicle stopped and rendered assistance. Orr had the good sense to be pole-axed by a reasonably wealthy and responsible Thai, and he paid her hospital bills.

Orr looked a mess, with a big black eye and bruises on her forehead, but was in good spirits and regaled me with all the troubles that had beset Lightning Jack's in the two months I'd been away. She said they were down to just eight or nine girls and although there were plenty of bar fines, the place was struggling to make ends meet.

Strangely, Grecian Ron had been the one to give Charlie the most trouble. He felt Peter was owed something since Charlie had managed to walk into a cheap bar, but when Charlie refused to give anything, Ron threatened to find a way of taking all the girls out of the bar.

One regular customer allegedly had a gun pointed at his head and was told to stay away from the bar.

A Filipino man had come in looking suspicious and tried to bar fine Jo, the new mamasan. He offered her 5,000 baht to go with him but she refused because she was unsure of the real reason behind the offer.

On a couple of occasions a Hong Kong Chinese man had come in asking for Peter and me. Orr also told me many people believed I received money for selling the bar to Charlie.

A day or so after talking with Orr, I ran into Mike who told me two Thai men with guns, who had come looking for Peter in Lightning Jack's, were linked to an Australian pair from the Northern Territory who had purchased his 50 percent stake in Cheerleaders A Go-Go earlier in the year. They failed to pay the rent and so Mike took the lease and sold the bar to a German. The Aussies had some high level Thai contacts, but so did Mike. They tried to have him arrested but failed because Mike had a 'get out of jail for free' card given to him by a higher-ranking Thai policeman he knew.

On a later visit to Pattaya, I went into the Anzac Hotel and Dang, the long-standing microwaveologist (cook was too good a word for the culinary disasters she served up) looked at me with some surprise and said, "I thought you were dead. Somebody tell me you got shot and were dead."

"The only thing that'll kill me Dang is your cooking," I replied.

A few months later, I went into Tahitian Queen A Go-Go and saw Nan's cousin Oom for the first time in a long while. She had been dancing at TQ for the previous two months. She looked at me in a strange way and said, "Someone tell me you die. You not dead, I'm so happy, I win."

I felt like a cat with nine lives although tales of my premature demise were fast reducing the number available to me.

The Good, the Bad and the Mentally Challenged

One of the great benefits of being involved in owning a bar in a place like Pattaya is you get to meet a wide variety of people, from the interesting, sensitive and intelligent (a rarity) to the wild, weird, and unclassifiable (more common).

One of the interesting characters was an American named Michael who was involved in the water purification business and had lived in Thailand since 1987. Considering the fact tap water in Thailand is pretty much undrinkable I would have thought he was sitting on a goldmine.

Michael said he lived in a huge house in Chiang Mai when he first arrived in the country. He advertised for a maid and interviewed a number of women for the position, finally settling on a beautiful 21-year-old who, he said, was, "dirt poor and didn't even understand 'hello'."

"She lived with her uncle because her parents had died and she was one of the most beautiful girls I had ever seen in my life," he told me.

"I spent a couple of weeks basically chasing her around the house and trying to get her to go out with me," he continued.

She eventually succumbed to Michael's charms and ministrations and agreed to go out with him.

"I took her virginity and she fell in love with me," he stated bluntly.

Three months later, he came to Pattaya for the first time to get away from Chiang Mai, intending to send for her.

"I had never seen anything like Pattaya and I became engrossed in the lifestyle so that instead of going back to Chiang Mai and getting her I just kept ringing and telling her to meet me," he said.

"She said her uncle and friends kept telling her Pattaya was a bad place and not to go and after three weeks of phone calls I just gave up."

One year later he went into a Thai bar/disco on Silom Road in Bangkok and "there she was, surrounded by clearly wealthy Thai men, dressed beautifully and complete with a nose job," Michael stated matter-of-factly.

"I didn't talk to her, I just walked out and left her to it," he said.

"Did she recognise you?" I asked.

"No, she didn't see me," he replied.

"Why didn't you try to get back with her or go and talk to her?" I asked.

"Because I liked the original girl, not the one she had obviously become," he answered.

Michael eventually came unstuck, borrowing money he could not afford to pay back and returned to the United States owing a lot of people and pursued by the local mafia.

***

One night an American wandered into Lightning Jack's and told me about a little tome called the *Asia File,* produced each year by people based in San Diego in the United States. The *Asia File* was a foreigner's guide to the best go-go bars and beer bars in places like Patpong Road, Soi Cowboy and Nana Plaza in Bangkok and the nightlife of Pattaya and Phuket, somewhat akin to a *Lonely Planet* guide to the sex trade. The authors gave each bar they visited a rating and told their readers the best aspect of the places they had frequented in the preceding 12 months.

The following night the American returned and gave me a photocopy of part of their most recent edition. It made interesting reading.

For example:

> 'All-night sounds much sexier than it usually is. Normally, it's a ride back to your hotel, showering separately, a too-quick fuck, several hours of 'sleeping together' while she clutches her protective towel. If in the morning she gets up, dresses, demands money or even hassles you for giving her 'only' B500, get rid of her and forget her. But if she fucks you a second time without your demanding it, you may have found a girl to go back to.'

The underlying theme of this work seemed to be the women working in the bars were nothing more than nameless, faceless, slant-eyed, brown-skinned whores whose duty it was to satisfy sex-hungry foreign predators without complaint and for as little remuneration as possible.

The relationship between bargirls and foreign men is one tinged with ambivalence. To the majority of Thai women the core relationships of their lives revolve around the family: mother, father, brothers, sisters, and children. Most foreigners cannot hope to come close to that sort of relationship. The problem unfortunately is so many men fool themselves and are beguiled into thinking they are indeed the focal point of a girl's life. Thinking in purely Western terms will simply drive the average foreigner crazy, and even those with an understanding of Thai culture still find it difficult to fathom.

The strength of the relationship between a mother and daughter in Thailand is not to be underestimated. Daughters generally want to marry and stay as close to their mothers as possible; mothers happily take on the role of baby-sitter and house-minder for their daughters. The girls who work in the go-go bars and beer bars of Bangkok and Pattaya traditionally spend time going home to see their parents, primarily their mothers. Strangely, the relationship between women and their mothers-in-law is usually nowhere near as close and convivial. Nice to think some things just don't change from culture to culture.

Of course, it takes a certain type of woman to become a prostitute in any country and at any time, although the capabilities exist for almost anyone faced with a bleak and desperate future to suspend their perception of morality. The cultural misunderstandings between foreign men and Thai women are exacerbated by the nature of the business of prostitution.

After complaining about the relatively poor performance of one of the girls he had taken from a go-go bar, the American author of the *Asia File* wrote, 'If one has the time/money to try a second time girls are known to loosen up.' Given human nature, it is probably not surprising.

A girl working in a bar, be it a beer bar or a go-go, gets used to going with men who only take her for one night before moving on to new conquests. If a man does decide to take her a second time, then of course the girl is more likely to show increased enthusiasm for the task. Especially if she happens to like the client.

"There is no problem bringing a lady to your hotel room in all except (maybe) the luxury resorts. Some of the really beautiful go-go girls may not be impressed by a cheap room, but beer bar girls don't mind..." Perhaps this gives a very sharp indication of the hierarchical nature of the international prostitution business in Thailand. However, I'm inclined to believe this is not necessarily the case, for there are many beautiful girls who work in beer bars and would never dream of working in a go-go. Moreover, some will ask as much, if not more, money than some go-go girls. Equally, there are girls working in go-go bars who really would be better off putting their clothes on and working out of beer bars.

In a discourse about the various charms of some bars in Bangkok, the writer of *Asia File* commented,

"Several of the girls have been on the game a long time and know every trick to get more money from you."

The *Asia File* has since changed its name and is now called *The Erotic Traveler*.

***

On the downside, one of the most boring persons I have ever had the misfortune to meet made his way into Lightning Jack's.

Adam* (not his real name) was an Englishman in his early thirties who worked as a carpenter for his father and had been to Pattaya a number of times. He was above average height with a lean build and short-cropped, receding, mousy-blonde hair. He rarely smiled and in some ways I felt sorry for him because he didn't have many friends and from his conversations it appeared his father was a bit of a domineering tyrant.

Unfortunately, he also had an arrogance characteristic of some people who are incredibly insecure but hide their insecurity with comments designed to make them feel superior to the rest of the human race.

One night in Lightning Jack's he surveyed the bar with a look of contempt for those who were there and stated, "I'm English [as if that automatically meant he was somehow superior] and I've got more intelligence than anyone else in this room." He didn't have the courtesy to add, 'present company excepted'.

He had been a regular resident of Cheena House (a guesthouse in Soi Skaw Beach) but moved out to a smaller room to co-habit with a 19-year-old Thai girl.

"I've had more women in Skaw Beach than anyone else," he boldly claimed. How he could possibly prove such a claim is anyone's guess and if it were true it just confirmed for me his personal insecurities.

I was downstairs with him in Cheena House one morning when he said to the manager, "I've had more women than anybody who has stayed at Cheena House haven't I Mr Suporn?"

"Yes, you always have different lady almost every night," confirmed a nonplussed Mr Suporn.

Despite his outward bravado, he was usually on the verge of, or in, a state of depression and anxiety.

One day I was walking down Skaw Beach Road when he joined me and asked if I would go to lunch with him. We went to the incongruously named Sailing Club. It's on Second Road and apart from not being anywhere near the water you can't even see water, unless it's the puddles in the road during the monsoon season.

I later went there one morning for the cheap 50-baht breakfast. Waitresses-five- outnumbered customers-three- with all the waitresses glued to the television watching a Thai movie. The breakfast came as advertised, although the bacon consisted of two thin strips from a seriously malnourished pig.

Adam was depressed because, he said, his girlfriend, "may not be in love with me. She's a pretty girl...but I love too much."

I noticed he had a black eye and to change the subject asked him how he'd come by it.

He looked sheepish and at first said he didn't want to tell me. I thought some foreigner had probably given him a back-hander but then he relented and said, "I got into a fight with a taxi driver."

He said he'd caught a baht bus at about 3:00 a.m. and when he got off at Skaw Beach he gave the driver five baht. The driver demanded 20 baht and Adam, who was drunk, told him to go to hell. The driver got out of the baht bus and belted Adam. I don't know if he coughed up the other 15 baht.

The black eye must have elicited sympathy from his circle of acquaintances because no sooner had it healed than he was sporting a second one. He wouldn't tell me for a couple of days how he had come about getting this second black eye. When he did, I wasn't really surprised.

"I was at home and the girl had gone out and I was feeling depressed, so I hit myself on the wardrobe door," he admitted.

***

Another person I met who came into Lightning Jack's for a drink was a Canadian soldier named Shannon. Tall and broad, he said he'd been part of the United Nations peacekeeping force in strife-torn Rwanda. Tribal fighting, leading to terrible genocide, had torn the country apart.

Shannon said the situation had been horrific and told me a tragic story about a five-year-old Rwandan orphan boy.

"We had gone into this orphanage and found that the water-well needed to be fixed. This little boy did his best to help us fix the well. It was a job which took us about 14 hours and when we left we gave the little fella some lollies for helping us. The next day we were called out to the orphanage again to fix the well. We had to drag that little boy's body out of the bottom of the well. The other kids had killed him so they could steal his lollies," Shannon told me with some emotion.

***

I didn't meet Alex, a solid shaven-headed 40-year-old Australian (originally from Melbourne), in the bar. I met him one evening in a small Thai restaurant in Bangkok. Although I quite liked him, he seemed to have become the quintessential bitter Thailand expatriate.

I was led to believe the man in this photo was the son of well-known English television personality Leslie Crowther. He certainly was English, had plenty of money to splash around and never once mentioned his antecedents: his parentage was whispered quietly by another bar owner who had nothing to gain by imparting such knowledge to a 'colonial' like me (who hadn't a clue who Leslie Crowther is or was).

"I've spent the last 15 years living in Asia, but I'm sick of it and I'm going home soon," he told me.

He had a five-year-old daughter named Karla but was separated from her mother (his new girlfriend was with him). The mother he said earned 14,000 baht a month in a job at the Marriott Hotel, but blew most of the money playing cards.

"She plays cards all day and all night when she is not working. She doesn't take care of my daughter. It's not the kind of life I want my daughter to have."

Alex's concern for his young daughter was evident throughout our conversation. It was clear she was the lynchpin of his life, the reason for his existence.

"I'm going to take my daughter to Australia with me. I'll probably go gold prospecting. I spent six weeks in an ashram in India with her. No meat, no eggs. Only vegetables and water and meditation. I came out weighing just 63 kilos."

He was now up around the 83-kilogram mark he said.

"I've lived in Pattaya and trained at the Universe Gym and the World Class Gym. I've had Thai girlfriends, but not the bargirl types. You know, I don't agree with Pauline Hanson, but Asians are just as racist- if that's the term you want to use- as us. I call it patriotism, not racism," Alex stated.

Pauline Hanson was an Australian politician, elected as an Independent, whose maiden speech to Parliament ignited a so-called 'race debate' in Australia. Her actions and comments had been widely reported in the Asian media. She lost her seat at the next election.

"Here in Thailand they don't want to sell to foreigners," Alex continued. "They say 'we have people who can't afford to buy land. If we let foreigners buy then the price of land will go up and even more Thais won't be able to afford to buy'. Look at Australia. Half of Queensland is owned by the Japanese and we have people in Australia who can't afford property."

In fact, Japanese owned a very small percentage of the state of Queensland real estate.

His thoughts on Thailand and Thai people were interesting. "You can never really count a Thai man as your friend. When it comes to the crunch, you are not ethnically the same. Thai men are very macho and they can't help but be jealous of us for a number of reasons."

Alex expounded on what these were. "First, the Thais, all Asians, black Africans and even our own Aborigines, think white skin is perfect. Whites make up seven percent of the world's population yet these people think white is great."

"Second, we're usually taller than the Thai men. Third, we're usually physically bigger. Even Asian body-builders usually don't get to the size that white Anglo-Saxon-type body builders do. Fourth, we have a bridge on our nose. It means we can wear any type of sunglasses we like. The Thais are always looking at a *farangs* nose and wishing theirs was the same. Fifth, we usually have more money than them and finally, we are supposed to have bigger dicks. Not that that matters or is even true, but it does concern them. They hate foreign men going into Thai-only brothels and screwing their women. They think the women will be stretched and won't be able to 'feel' a Thai man after a foreigner's been with her."

You Not Believe My Story

Many of the girls who have been working in the bars for long enough will tell the most amazing stories about their lives. Most of them will give you one version and when you come back a few days later they will have forgotten the original story and tell a new and possibly more truthful version.

Hew was a classic example of the bargirl 'sob' story. I met Hew when she was working in a go-go bar in Naklua. She told me she was 22 and came originally from Khorat. For dancing topless, she was paid 6,000 baht a month and for performing the dart shows received an extra 2,000 baht a month. Hew claimed she hadn't been working in bars for very long.

She said her brothers and sisters were all younger and her mother had serious eye problems. The "my mother/father/sister/brother needs an eye operation" is one of the oldest sob scams used by bargirls.

A few days later I returned to the bar but Hew only vaguely remembered me. This time she said she had been working in go-go's for five years and had a four and-a-half-year old son to a former German boyfriend. She had been to Germany but her boyfriend left her after four years. She claimed she still loved him.

She then said her father died when she was two years old and, surprise, surprise, her mother had died when Hew was 10 years old. The eye problem must have been deadly serious.

***

At a beer bar in *Soi* 8, I spoke with a 19-year-old girl named Noot. Over the next few days, I came to know her better and she said she'd once had a German boyfriend for two months and been pregnant to him. However, she'd had a motorbike accident when she was two months pregnant and lost the baby. That was her first version of the story.

A little later, she confessed she'd actually had an abortion when she and the German split up. She also told me she was only 18 years old, not 19. Noot told me her siblings consisted of one younger brother, an older sister and older brother (both married to Thais).

Noot told me she was staying in the bar for a short time and would then go to school in Bangkok. When I came back a few months later Noot was still in the bar. I took her for something to eat and asked her why she hadn't gone to school in Bangkok.

"Lazy," she replied.

She then claimed her father was in debt to the tune of 100,000 baht and she wanted to work the bar until the debt was paid off. Her father, of course, didn't know she was working a bar.

"When I pay the money I will go home and stay," she said.

She was waiting for an older Italian man, her "boyfriend", to come and see her.

I lost touch with her until late one night, about four years later, when she saw me. She claimed to have gone home to Buriram for a time but had been in and out of a series of relationships over the past few years. She was sporting a tattoo on her right shoulder and had a belly ring. She was also dressing better, her English was excellent, and was still working in bars.

***

An attractive 21-year-old, when Lek first came down to Pattaya she got a job at Cheena House cleaning rooms.

Originally from Ubon she told me she had a five-year-old daughter who was at home being looked after by her sister. She left Cheena House and went to work in a beer bar in *Soi* 8 but then became a freelancer and started working in the taxi hire place located next door to Cheena House, at a wage of 3,000 baht a month. She claimed she only went to the bar when she needed money.

Lek had an older brother, two younger sisters and a young brother. Her parents ran a food stall in Ubon but her elder brother didn't work, "him crazy," she said.

She said she was 14 when she came down to work in Bangkok. At 15, she met a 27-year-old Thai man who wanted to go out with her. Lek claimed she got drunk one night and the man virtually raped her and made her pregnant. She and her family went to the police but the man paid a 20,000 baht bribe and escaped going to jail.

She said the police gave her just 4,000 baht. Lek later married and went to live in Germany.

***

I met Sakorn, then 20 years old, when she was dancing in Honey A Go-Go. From Sukothai, she was tall, with lustrous long straight hair and an attractive face. She had a four-year-old daughter, spoke good English and had been in Pattaya for three years. I asked her if she had a long-term foreign boyfriend.

"Yes. I am in love with an American soldier. He is in the Marines. He is a sergeant and when he comes to see me I stop work and stay with him," she told me.

"How often do you see him?" I asked.

"He comes three times every year and stays for about two months. But I'm not happy with him. He stays with me in my room, I cook for him and clean and take care of him but he doesn't give me anything because he says he has no money."

Her room cost her 1,800 baht a month and the only way she could get the money was to go with men.

She was able to get any man she wanted yet was in love with this American, despite his nonchalant attitude towards her. I told her she should dump him and look for somebody better. She took my advice and became involved with a Finnish man for a week or so.

As it happened, the Marine turned up in Pattaya unannounced a little later and came to see Sakorn. She hadn't gone to work that night, as she was feeling sick. She told me later, "I left him alone, I didn't touch him and didn't care that I had pictures of other men around my room. He could see I had changed and he started to be better to me. Now we're engaged." She showed me a decent-sized engagement ring and told me he was sending her 15,000 baht a month to stop work. They later married and seemed extremely happy together.

Sakorn said her father died when she was 12, leaving her mother to bring up four children by herself. She said her 23-year-old sister had worked in the Pattaya bars about four or five years previously.

"She had a baby and I looked after it. In three months, she only sent 1,500 baht home. Now I send sometimes 7,000 baht, this month I send 4,000 baht but she complains I don't send enough," Sakorn told me.

"I want to send the money to my mother but I have to send to my sister because my mother doesn't have a bank account. My older brother is addicted to *ganja* [marijuana], my other brother is OK but his girlfriend is no good."

It seemed like prostitution was a family business because the next time I came to Thailand she introduced me to her 19-year-old cousin who had come down to start work in the bars.

***

Toy, one of the service girls in Lightning Jack's, was 34 years old. A friendly and attractive lady supporting a young daughter, she told me she was receiving 27,000 baht a month from three different men: an American, an Austrian and a Dutchman. All of who no doubt thought they were her one and only true love.

The American and Austrian each sent her 10,000 baht a month while the Dutchman *only* sent her 7,000 baht a month.

When he- the Dutchman- sent her an airline ticket to go and stay with him in the Netherlands, she asked me if she could get off the plane in Frankfurt. I told her she couldn't; she had to complete the journey.

"Why do you want to get off in Frankfurt?" I asked her.

"I don't like the Dutch man very much, I want to go see Austrian man," she replied.

"Why don't you like the Dutchman?" I asked.

"He's a Cheap Charlie," she replied.

"But he sends you 7,000 baht a month," I said.

"Yes, but the others send me 10,000," she countered.

She was quite happy to accept the Dutchman's money but because he gave less than the other two she saw him as cheap.

***

Cha, our DJ, had a girlfriend named Sao who worked as a dancer in the bar. It didn't seem to bother him that his girlfriend would go off and have sex with foreigners. After Lightning Jack's closed down Cha went to work in another go-go bar and Sao went with him. I saw them a couple of years later and Cha said they now had a son. Later that same night I saw Sao in the go-go bar sitting with a German man, "my boyfriend, I know him long time" she told me. He was in Thailand for a few weeks and would take her everywhere and buy clothes for her; blissfully unaware of the fact the DJ at her bar was also her long-time boyfriend and the father of her child. I don't know what story she gave the German man to explain the existence of her baby, that is if she told him at all. I do know some years later I saw Cha working as a DJ in a go-go bar in Soi Cowboy in Bangkok and he told me he and Sao had split up. Hardly surprising really. He later returned to Pattaya to work as the DJ in the Pretty Girl A Go-Go (now Nui's 2 A-Go-Go).

***

The cast of characters who came to work in the bar ranged across the spectrum. From very pretty young girls with attitude to more sedate ladies they were a mixed bunch and some of the girls managed to acquire nicknames, usually given to them by customers.

For example, there was Kai. We named her 'Bruiser'. She was very tall and possessed a strong, fit body (because, she said, "I work out in the 'yim' nearly every day") and a head like a robber's dog. I told people she wasn't a dancer she was our bouncer.

One of the most popular girls, in terms of being bar-fined, was 20-year-old Wi. A small, petite, "fucking machine" (her words) she had a 21-year-old Thai boyfriend who worked in a boy's go-go bar. She told me they were going to work for a couple of years and would save as much money as they could before getting out and getting married. An apparently 'lazy' right eye caused Dave, a Scottish expatriate who later opened a popular beer bar called The Kennel, to christen her Clarence, after the cross-eyed lion that featured in the 1970s TV series *Daktari*. Wi did leave the bar a few months later and I never saw her again.

Van, a pretty 21-year-old dancer who worked at Cheerleaders (which I was managing at the time) had a Thai boyfriend who she wanted to marry within the next three years. She had been with him for three years and he worked as a bar boy at Blackout A Go-Go (now Living Dolls Showcase A Go-Go).

We also employed a pretty 21-year-old virgin as a service girl (although both her sisters were 'working girls'). She was constantly asked out by customers but refused to go with them.

A number of girls who work in go-go bars begin their 'careers' in the business of prostitution as virgins. At one stage, we had a pair of sisters who had come down from the country to work as dancers. The younger sister also proved to be a virgin and after dancing for her required time would come off stage and hide in a corner. One night I jokingly told her a man had paid to take her out of the bar-she almost fainted. In the month she worked at the bar she never went with a customer.

Her elder sister had been pregnant and had an abortion that put her father into debt and the sisters had come to Pattaya to earn enough money to clear the impost. The younger sister worked for just one month and then returned home while the elder girl stayed on.

You've Got to Lick It Before You Kick It

On 23 October 1996, the Sydney *Daily Telegraph* newspaper ran the following small story:

Aussie murder arrest

A tourist has been arrested over the stabbing murder of a 50-year-old Australian man in the Thai seaside beach resort town of Pattaya.

An Australian Embassy official said Anthony Brady was stabbed during an argument with the 55-year-old French man.

The official said the embassy was still waiting on details from the Thai police.

The murder happened at a seaside bungalow in south Pattaya, 150km from Bangkok.

Local police were alerted to a fight at the bungalow and arrived as the Frenchman was stabbing Mr Brady.

Police took Mr Brady to the Pattaya Memorial Hospital, where he was pronounced dead on arrival.

I arrived back in Thailand a couple of weeks later, went straight to Pattaya and down to the Anzac Hotel. Ron was not there but the waitresses told me a German, not a Frenchman, had stabbed Tony. The German was apparently a local expatriate drunk and knew Tony on a casual basis. He was asking Tony for money, Tony refused, they began arguing and the German stabbed him.

I could think of many expatriates in Pattaya who I could envisage coming to an untimely and violent death, but Tony was not among them. He had married an ex-go-go dancer, taken on her child and still owned a three-bedroom unit in his old hometown of Perth in Western Australia.

Ron later put up a framed colour photograph of Tony and placed it over the corner where Tony could be always be found, reading the paper, doing the cryptic crossword, having one of his million or so smokes or a chat with his friends.

A brief article in the Sydney *Daily Telegraph* of 7 January 1997 headlined, 'Deadly sex trap sprung' caused me to recall an incident that occurred to my friend Martin.

Filing from Bangkok the reporter stated:

'Police at Thailand's Pattaya beach resort said yesterday they had arrested six people for allegedly robbing male tourists after enticing them to lick the drug-laced nipples of female suspects.

Police said five Thai women and a man were arrested on charges of drugging and robbing tourists following a long investigation prompted by the deaths of dozens of victims by suspicious drug overdoses.

Police at Pattaya, about 180 km southeast of Bangkok, said the suspects confessed to having applied drugs to the nipples of female members of the robbery gang.

They then lured victims into licking their breasts, causing them to pass out in a few minutes.

At least 45 western and Asian tourists had died of drug overdoses at Pattaya in the past year.'

"I've been robbed," said a slurred voice.

A tattooed, muscular figure, wrapped only in a towel, literally staggered into my room in Cheena House, in Soi Skaw Beach.

It was 10:00 a.m. and I was talking with Manchester Dave, who also had a room in Cheena House, about our plans for the day ahead, when we were suddenly disturbed by Martin's arrival.

We both looked around in stunned surprise as he stumbled through the door, reeling like an alcoholic awoken from a nightmare. He was clearly unwell, pale and barely able to remain upright.

"What happened?" I said.

"Come and look at my room... It's a mess... She robbed me," he muttered, almost incoherently.

The three of us walked- well two of us walked while the other stumbled- down the hallway to Martin's room. The place was a shambles. It looked as if an errant gibbon had gone berserk in the confines of the room. His large suitcase had been prised open and anything of value pilfered. The room had been searched quite thoroughly.

Martin wore two gold chains around his neck, a gold wristlet and gold ring and these were all missing.

We were soon joined in the room by Martin's nephew, Jason and his friend. Both were on their first trip to Thailand.

Dave said, in his broad Manchester brogue, "Tell us what happened Martin. Who did this to you?"

"Well, I went up to *Soi* 2 last night and was sitting at this bar having a drink when a very beautifully dressed and pretty lady sat down just near me," Martin said. "I was laughing and joking with all the girls at the bar, as I do, you know."

Martin was well known among the outside beer bars of northern Pattaya and well liked by the girls for his sense of fun and humour.

"Then I got talking to this girl, I bought her a drink and asked her name. She told me she was 22 years old and was a hairdresser and she was just down from Bangkok for the weekend," Martin continued. "She was dressed really beautifully and I thought 'there's no way she's going to go for me.' And her English was very good."

"After having a drink at the bar in *Soi* 2 I asked her what she was doing and she said 'I'll go with you'. I was a bit surprised but we went down to Leo's bar in *Soi* 9. All the girls said 'hello' to me and we spoke to them. She could see that a lot of people knew me. I don't know what the time was when we came back here. I think around two o'clock. She came out of the bathroom with her towel wrapped around her waist. She had a beautiful body. Then she said 'Kiss me, Martin' and I kissed her. She gave me a deep tongue kiss, and that's when she must have slipped me the drug. I don't remember anything until I woke up this morning. My left eye is really sore. She must have poked me in the eye to make sure I was really out of it."

His left eye was indeed puffy and partially bloodshot.

"I think we should go to the police and report this," I said.

"OK. Let me get dressed and I'll meet you downstairs."

Some 20 minutes later, he came downstairs and, because he was still very unsteady on his feet, we arranged for a taxi to take us to the main police station, located on Beach Road.

After talking with a couple of junior policemen, we were asked to wait and a more senior officer would attend to the matter. After about half an hour a tall, handsome, 30-something, casually-dressed police officer interviewed Martin and took down the details of the incident.

Martin appeared incoherent and very vague when answering some of the questions. This was obviously because the drug had left his system in some disarray and made him appear intoxicated. We established the value of the gold and other items at over 140,000 baht. She had also absconded with about 13,000 baht in cash. Not bad for a night's work.

Martin gave a description of the girl: brown eyes and black hair. That narrowed the search down to around 30 million possibilities.

Of course, the description was a little more detailed than that. She had short black hair and was of average height, attractive and well dressed. Maybe the search could be narrowed down to just a few million people.

It took Martin until the early evening before he started to feel well again. He had been to Thailand on many occasions and never had any trouble of this nature. "Here I am with my nephew and his mate and I'm constantly warning them to be careful, and I'm the one who gets done over," he remarked wryly.

The incident left him terribly disillusioned and he said, "I don't think I'll come back here again, I think I might go home early."

However, within a day or so he had regained most of his former good humour and said he'd be back again, probably within six months.

"Why should I let one girl and one bad incident spoil my love for this place?"

When we related this incident to David, the proprietor of Joffens, a small restaurant along Second Road where we habitually ate breakfast, he told us this was the third time something like this had happened to someone he knew in the past six months.

Martin returned to England a few days later but continued to come back to the 'Land of Smiles' on a regular basis, eventually marrying a Thai lady and settling down in Pattaya.

It was not the last time people I knew being robbed in similar fashion. Despite the arrests of the six people in January 1997, I heard of two further incidents occurring after that time.

An Australian friend of mine, staying at Cheena House, came to see me one morning and said he'd been robbed of about 25,000 baht. He said he'd been wandering along Beach Road at about 3:00 a.m. when approached by two girls. They offered to both go with him and he accepted. After the double act they said, "We go in the morning?" He said OK and then fell asleep. When he woke up at 6:30 a.m., they were gone and he'd been robbed.

A few days later, another Australian said he had taken two girls back to his room early in the morning and woke up to find himself considerably lighter in the wallet.

It was like the hunter unwittingly becoming the hunted.

To Be or Not to Be

A general election had been called and the night before the people were to go to the polls, all the go-go bars in Pattaya and Bangkok were closed. How the closing of bars frequented mainly by foreigners who couldn't give a toss which party managed to corrupt enough people to win an election was going to help in the free and orderly process of voting for candidates was beyond the comprehension of most people in Pattaya.

If the idea was to give the working girls, taxi drivers and food sellers a chance to get a good nights' sleep before making their vital mark upon a ballot paper then the exercise was a failure. People were out in force around the streets and most of the girls who wanted too were on the prowl, safe in the knowledge they didn't have to entice potential customers to part with bar fines.

As well as the go-go's, the beer bars were also supposed to be closed. However, most of them were open but, in accordance with the rules, were not selling alcohol; at least not openly. Instead, beer and spirits were being served in teacups and coffee mugs. There was no music or live bands and lights in the bars were turned down or off. With the go-go's shut the dancers were forced to look for business on the dimly lit streets.

With the neon bright lights subdued, I strolled down Beach Road to see what was, or wasn't, happening.

I walked past many bars, drank in a couple and then decided to look for something to eat. I saw a short girl with slightly frizzy shoulder-length dark hair and wearing a large red and black T-shirt and white shorts, waiting to buy a pancake from a roadside stall. From behind, she had great legs. She also had a nice face. I smiled at her and introduced myself. She smiled back from a small, delicate mouth. I spoke to her in Thinglish, my usual mixture of

Thai and English, and after ascertaining her name, "Be", I found out she was 19 and had arrived in Pattaya to work in a bar about a month earlier.

Be originally hailed from the north-eastern city of Khon Kaen but had been working in an office in Bangkok for the previous four years, earning 8,500 baht a month- a fairly reasonable wage.

A year earlier, while out shopping in her local supermarket one day, she met a 22-year-old New Zealander. He asked her out. She accepted and within a short time fell in love with him. He was her first lover, but the relationship held a major problem in that he was married to a 38-year-old Thai lady. His wife soon found out about the relationship and on one occasion confronted Be, her husband's *mia noi.*

"I win; she small lady and I win," was how Be described the obviously physical encounter.

Be and I talked at her bar for a while, she had character and intelligence and I liked her. I asked her if she wanted to come with me and play some pool at the Manhattan Cafe in south Pattaya. She accepted and we spent an hour or so at the pool table.

We then went for something to eat at the Kiss restaurant on Second Road before going back to my room in Cheena House. Be turned on the television, sat on the end of the bed and removed her shoes.

"I show you a picture of my boyfriend," she said producing her wallet and showing me a picture of her ex-lover. Staring back at me was a tall, handsome, well-built blond man dressed in a singlet and running shorts and holding a cricket bat. His face was creased with an engaging smile. No wonder she'd fallen in love with him. Be was an attractive girl without being especially pretty and she would have viewed him as a good 'catch', at least in the 'looks' department.

Be looked longingly at the photo and whispered his name a few times, repeating, "why, why, why?"

She then showed me an address book with his name and address in Auckland, New Zealand. She was clearly upset and still very much in love with him.

"I told him if he ever break up with me I would go to Pattaya to work in bar and find *farang*," she said.

"He took me to Pattaya one time before and when I told him what I would do he said that was very bad," she continued.

Be got up and went into the bathroom for a couple of minutes, came out, sat on the bed and started putting her shoes back on saying, "I go home; I'm sorry. I think I not stay in Pattaya too long."

She told me she'd only gone with one other foreigner since she started working in the bar and been unable to sleep with him because of her feelings for her ex-boyfriend. I felt sympathetic and told her I'd walk her home. She lived just three or four minutes away from me.

"What are you doing for money if you're not going with men?" I asked her.

"Before I left Bangkok I had saved up a bit of money and I'm living on that at the moment," she replied.

I told her she should go back to Bangkok as soon as possible because this was not the 'job' for her.

"You cannot let a foreigner pay the bar for you, take you out and then not stay with him. I don't mind, I understand how you feel, but some men might get angry."

I told her another foreigner might go back to the bar and demand his bar fine back and this would give her a lot of trouble.

She told me, "I only ever wanted to have one man. If I know man good to me, don't smoke, don't drink whisky, then I can go with him, but I can't do like this."

I left her outside the entrance to her apartment and said she could come and visit me if she wanted. I knew she probably wouldn't and hoped she would go back to work in a normal situation in Bangkok and not stay in Pattaya. Maybe she took my advice, as I never saw her again.

Boys will be Boys

In a 10-year study conducted from 1938 to 1948 and entitled *Sexual Behaviour in the Human Male*, Dr Alfred Kinsey found an incredible 37 percent of the male population would experience at least one homosexual experience to the point of orgasm at some time in their lives. Given that homosexuality in many countries is no longer considered a criminal activity, the percentage may now well be higher.

The reality is that desire is a lot more complicated than just genitalia. Many psychologists and sex researchers have a belief that humans desire certain types of people rather specific genders. It is not the genitalia that is paramount but the person.

For a great many years, the Land Dyaks of Sarawak, also known as the Iban, adopted a unique style of homosexuality. A group of young boys, selected from early youth to be trained as healers and exorcists, would dress in female attire, marry men, and live in the communal longhouse as women. Known as *mamang bali,* they were a very real example of an attitude to human sexuality completely at variance with the accepted norms of allegedly sophisticated Western culture.

Homophobia, as with racism, is not a rational emotion, feeding on ignorance to produce hatred and discrimination. Thailand has probably one of the world's most enlightened attitudes to homosexuality with little evidence of homophobia. Homosexuals, transsexuals and transvestites (known collectively by the Thai word *katoey*) are a common sight, even in out-of-the-way country towns and villages. Most have no trouble finding employment and being accepted in society, even if only on the surface. In areas of the public sector, and in academia, homophobia is more likely to be found.

Pattaya has probably the largest per capita concentration of *katoeys* in the country. Some are hard-working, others are performers in shows like Alcazar and Tiffany's while still others dance in girl go-go's, work in beer bars, and a large number walk the streets as freelancers on the Beach and Second Roads.

Some are not much more than common thieves, preying on single males, mugging them in the street while others go with punters back to their hotel rooms and make off with everything, including the family jewels.

Katoeys are generally easy to spot. They are all 300 centimetres tall. OK, that's in high heel shoes, but what I can't figure is why, when the shoes are removed, most are still more than a few centimetres taller than the average male.

The Tiffany's and Alcazar Shows are usually packed out every night of the week for their cabarets while a bar called the Malibu does a pretty good series of amateur performances.

Imagine the Ziegfeld Follies with balls and you get an idea what these cabaret shows are all about. All feathers and sequins, lip-synching their way through a series of supposedly well-rehearsed routines. Unfortunately, on too many occasions the routines look like they could do with the services of a sergeant major from the Coldstream Guards to knock them into some semblance of organised rhythm.

The other limiting factor is many of the performers prance around the stage looking as though they've had a sharp object deftly inserted in a place where the sun doesn't shine and all they can do to ease the discomfort is flail their arms like an ostrich on heat.

For a real on-the-street glimpse of the lady-boys, the nightly Simon Cabaret (now closed down) on Walking Street, used to be just the ticket for those who wanted to avoid the crowds of Chinese, Japanese and Koreans who make up the bulk of the audience for Alcazar and Tiffany's.

Couples out strolling along Walking Street between 9:00 p.m. to 10:00 p.m. were treated to a number of the performers, decked out in their finest and gaudiest costumes, lolling about on the pavement and chatting with passers by. Just how many rolls of film were gone through by supposedly well-adjusted people having their photos taken with people they would normally avoid like the plague would have made an interesting study in social anthropology.

***

One of the draw cards of the sex industry in Thailand for homosexual foreigners is the general acceptance of their predilection and the fact homosexuality is not illegal.

Pattaya is one of the favoured destinations around the world for gay men and boasts a large number of go-go bars catering especially to males. In fact, the place fairly squeals with them.

The first time I came to Pattaya, I wandered into the main gay centre of the city by accident. The street in question is just off Second Road and as I turned the corner from Pattayaland Soi 2 and saw the sign, 'Boyztown' straddling the roadway, I took a closer look at my surroundings. All the bars contained men, both Thai and foreigners, although clearly the Thais were there for the business of providing foreigners with pleasure.

Pattaya has a number of areas that are recognised as predominantly gay. Marina and Sunee Plaza's, Pattayaland Soi 1 (somewhat gender-confused as it has plenty of bars with female workers) and Soi 3 (Boyztown) and part of the three soi's known colloquially as Day-Night are the main sections housing gay go-go bars, beer bars, and restaurants.

The Boy go-go bars are staffed by young males who- as with their female counterparts- are available for sex at a price. A lot of the men working in the male bars are not homosexual. It is generally accepted that some 30 percent of the males working in these places are 'straight' and another 40 percent bi-sexual. For many boys, going with foreign men for money is just another job and quite a few have Thai girlfriends, many working in the female go-go and beer bars. Foreign women can often be seen entering the boy bars and picking up a man for the night; some even form long-term relationships.

A number of the outside beer bars employ one or two *katoeys*. At one bar in *Soi* 9 I knew a lady-boy named Apple. I asked 'her' to take me on a short guided tour around a couple of the Boy go-go's.

Apple was 21-years-old, tall with an attractive face. 'She' was essentially a cross-dresser rather than a transsexual. At the time I knew her, Apple had just started taking the necessary hormones to make her breasts grow and was hoping to save enough money to get the 'cut'. She told me her German boyfriend was going to give her 100,000 baht to have the operation to remove the unwanted male appendage.

Sadly, Apple had deformed hands, the result of an accident to her fingers when she was just five months old. She was unable to straighten the fingers of either hand and had trouble gripping various objects.

Apple needed some money from a friend who worked in a Boy go-go bar so we went there first. Inside, the bar looked very similar to the girls' go-go bars. On stage were six or seven young Thai males dancing, very poorly, in their underwear. Apple borrowed 500 baht from her friend and took me to another boy bar where she said, "They have shows." I dreaded to think what kind of shows they were, but acquiesced as I had embarked on a mission to gain a first-hand insight into the 'alternative' nightlife of Pattaya. At least that's my story!

The bar, called the Gentleman's Club, was very similar to the one we had just left, although smaller. On stage were about six Thai men, all of them I judged to be in their early twenties. Spread around the bar were plenty of men who looked and sounded European, most seemed to be in their late forties and fifties and were generally overweight.

When a young blond-headed European man came into the bar and took a seat, three or four of the young Thai boys immediately surrounded him. Just like the girls in the go-go's, as soon as a physically alluring customer entered a bar he was 'set upon' by workers looking to spend the night with someone physically attractive for a change.

The floorshows consisted of one boy, body-painted to look like an Australian Aboriginal preparing for an initiation ceremony, performing a public masturbation. The lights were dimmed; he grabbed hold of himself, closed his eyes and 'tugged' away in slow motion. He took a long, long time to finally ejaculate and I wouldn't mind betting he was thinking of his girlfriend as he stroked away.

Meanwhile, so as not to bore the audience, two boys came onto the stage and gave each other a head job. After doing this for a couple of minutes one boy mounted the other and proceeded, thankfully with a condom applied, to give the other anal intercourse.

Another act consisted of boys getting live goldfish and slowly releasing these squirming denizens of the deep from their rectums into a bowl of water. It's lucky goldfish have a memory span of just three seconds, otherwise I hate to think of the psychological trauma they might have suffered.

Another boy got his 'jollies' by squatting over the end of the stage and easing eggs, one at a time, from his anal tract into a wine glass, a number of them cracking on impact. I've never looked at scrambled eggs the same since.

After each of these little shows, the participants would come around the crowd asking for a tip, something that rarely happens in the girl go-go bars after a stage show.

Apple and I left after the show and I thanked her for her time. I was to see her a few more times over the next year or so and it was evident the hormones were working well as her breasts grew. To the best of my knowledge, she eventually went off to Germany to stay with her boyfriend.

Money for Nothing, and Your Chicks for Free

There are many foreigners whose experience of Thailand is limited to interactions with what might be termed the lower stratum of society: bargirls, peasants, taxi drivers, hotel employees and the like. They complain these Thais always seem to have their hands outstretched for money. The foreigner is always asked to pay for everything.

While this is a generally true statement and can therefore cloud the judgement with regard to how foreigners view Thai people, there is definitely another side to the story.

Jimmy, Janet's cousin and his Thai friends, were businesspeople whose income was certainly higher than average. In fact, their income was probably higher than many foreigners.

On a drive back from Pattaya to Bangkok one evening, Jimmy looked at me, smiled and, patting me on the leg, said "massage." I was hoping he meant, "Let's go to a massage place" rather than offering to give me a personal introduction to the art.

Thankfully, the former is exactly what he meant and once we hit Bangkok he took me to one of the plushest brothels I had ever seen. Called Victoria's Secrets it was housed in a three-storey pseudo-Victorian-Gothic mansion. Very beautiful young ladies greeted us as we walked through the door and we were shown to a nice restaurant where we partook of a sumptuous feast. Had we so desired we could have repaired to a private room to take our supper and be entertained by another beautiful hostess and by porno movies on the TV, or gone to play snooker or pool on one of the many tables in another room.

After dinner Jimmy took me out to the 'goldfish bowl' where girls attired in evening gowns with numbers pinned on them sat behind a big window waiting to be picked to go upstairs and give a customer a 'massage'.

He told me to pick a girl. I don't like just 'picking' a number in the same way you choose a dish from a Chinese menu but there wasn't much else I could do so I selected Number 144. Her name was Noot and she spoke no English. I ascertained she came from the Isaan region. I was unable to determine what kind of massage diploma she had obtained, although I suspected Shiatsu and Swedish were not words with which she would be familiar. A 25-year-old, Noot said she'd been in Bangkok for six years and had been working at Victoria's Secrets for the previous eight months and I was her first *farang*.

After cleaning my ears out with a cotton bud while running a warm bath she then got undressed. I followed suit and we both got into the large bathtub. She rubbed soap and oil into me and when we came out about 10 minutes later I felt squeaky clean and ready for...a good night's sleep.

Noot emptied the bath, got out, gathered up a towel and dried me before drying herself. She guided me onto the bed where we experimented with a bit of horizontal folk dancing, something at which Noot was quite proficient.

After we'd finished I met up with Jimmy and his two friends for something to eat in a private room where a pretty young hostess with the appropriate name of Porn joined us. The cost of all this was borne by Jimmy and his mates: my bill was at least 3,000 baht all up, more money than I would spend in an average day in Thailand. I did not pay a single baht, for the food, drink or massage and I knew not to offer.

In Thailand the person who has invited you to eat, or, in this case, have a massage, pays. In the hierarchical nature of society, the burden of superior status and respect costs a lot of money. The foreigner is generally perceived by the peasantry and bargirls to be superior and therefore the fact they expect you to pay for almost everything is as natural as night following day.

Where people of similar status get together, you will still find one person will pay the bill for the whole group. In this way, the person gathers about him more status and respect. It is expected that at some later stage the favour will be returned.

***

The night after Victoria's Secrets, Jimmy took me out with his brother and a friend to the newly-opened Phoebus Amplitheatre, a nightclub/disco located opposite the Fortune Hotel. We met Jimmy's well-heeled mates out the front of the disco.

Membership cost 10,000 baht. For that amount of money, a member received 20 bottles of Johnny Walker whisky and free mixers such as soda and Coca Cola or Pepsi. The booze was kept in the club and brought out each time a member attended the disco. When the 20 bottles had been consumed, membership could either be renewed at 10,000 baht or whisky bottles could be purchased individually at 2,400 baht a pop.

Phoebus seemed to have the world's biggest disco and light show and looked like something out of the movie *Battlestar Galactica*. It had a large stage where a band performed every night, and between each bracket there was disco music and a laser light show.

The roof looked akin to a NASA Space Station, peppered with thousands of multi-coloured lights, while the surrounding galleries rose for four flights with seating for hundreds of people in each. Reputed to have cost 100 million baht to build, it turned over at least 1 million baht per night and was always busy. We attended on a Tuesday night and the place was packed to the rafters.

It was the ritual of the lavatory I found most amusing.

Number 144 from the Victoria's Secrets massage parlour in Bangkok. A thorough professional.

Answering the call of nature I ascertained the location of the gents and sauntered off to take a leak. I found a whole army of young men, dressed very neatly, waiting to direct me towards a urinal which would satisfy my every taste.

I found what I hoped would be a quiet spot to point an inhibited Percy at the porcelain. Just after taking aim I sensed a uniformed navvy at my left shoulder. I surmised he was hoping to get a sneak peek at a foreign penis, but instead he applied a hot towel firmly on the back of my neck. He started to massage my neck, a ritual he no doubt thought would aid in the free flow of liquid from my nether regions. I continued emptying my bladder and, satisfied, I zipped up my jeans with as much decorum as I could muster. Proceeding to the basin to wash my hands my neck-massaging lackey turned on the tap (maybe he thought I was some sort of Neanderthal incapable of operating such intricate machinery) and dried my hands with yet another towel (I'd hate to see the laundry bill for this joint) while another character fell to his knees and started to massage my right leg, moving slowly up my thigh. I put a stop to all this by pulling out a 100-baht note and watched their collective eyes light up. I deposited it on the youth nearest the exit and made my escape. I resolved not to return to the lavatory again that night if I could possibly help it. Having given such a large tip for what most people took to be normal service I thought next time they might start the leg massage further north of the knee that I'd like.

A few days later Janet and Jimmy came down to Pattaya and, with three others, I accompanied them to a Karaoke bar in a posh hotel near Jomtien beach. We arrived just after 2:00 a.m. and found ourselves in the middle of a birthday party for one of Pattaya's leading law enforcement officers.

The policeman paid the band an extra 5,000 baht to continue until he was ready to go home, which turned out to be 6:00 a.m. We drank, we danced, we ate, we sang songs, and then we drank some more, danced some more, and ate some more until we had completely milked all the fun we were going to have out of the place. Since it was a karaoke bar, the policeman and his guests took turns murdering, sorry, singing, Thai songs. Then, at one point, the police chief asked the band to play some English-language rock and roll- especially for the *farang*. We even did a duet together of Kris Kristofferson's 'Help Me Make It Through The Night', although I have to say his rendition of the duet was far more impressive than my contribution.

At the conclusion of the evening the police chief not only paid his- no doubt large- bill but also coughed up for most of our bill, although Jimmy did kick in 2,000 baht.

***

A couple of years later I was in Udon Thani staying with a family who owned a number of gold shops. On the first night they took me to a place called the Sleep Inn for an evening of karaoke singing. The Sleep Inn was a motel as well as a karaoke bar and when we eventually left at about two in the morning I thought it was wasn't particularly well named, as I couldn't imagine anyone getting much sleep in the place.

There were eight of us, me being the only foreigner, and we were given our own private room. Actually, it put me in mind of a padded cell. The room contained a large television and sequencer for keying in the karaoke songs as well as two long upholstered benches for seating and a low table for snacks and the inevitable whisky and beer bottles. The main feature of the small room was the padding around the walls. It was obviously designed to keep the noise emanating from the room to a minimum, except I couldn't help wondering when the guards were going to come in and strap us into straightjackets and administer sedatives.

We were given a folder with all the songs we could sing and some were listed in English. All the Thais requested 'Hotel California' by *The Eagles* but I found the funniest entry was 'Hark! The Herald Angels *Sin*'.

Once again, I was not asked to contribute to the expense of the night and indeed over the next few days I found it almost impossible to spend any money.

Don't give up your day job. Many nighttime security guards work during the day, so it's hardly surprising a number find it difficult to remain alert in the wee small hours. (photo from *Bangkok World,* 1971)

Mad Max vs Bangkok Traffic

Bangkok, the former 'Venice of the East' as it was known for some decades earlier this century because its canals (*khlongs*) were reminiscent of that grand old Italian city, is more like a sibling of Los Angeles these days. In the name of progress, many *khlongs* were filled in and cemented over to make way for roads.

Unfortunately, no one seems to have explained to the Bangkok city fathers that filling in the *khlongs* of a city located in a low-lying area tends to turn the annual monsoon season into the 'how-high-will-the-floodwaters-reach-this-year' Olympics in the downtown areas of the bustling metropolis.

Recognised as climatically one of the hottest cities in the world, it is not a pedestrian or walker-friendly place. In the side streets, pavements are virtually non-existent, forcing pedestrians onto the verges of the roadway and rendering them at the mercy and diligence of oncoming cars and motorbikes. Where pavements do exist, they are rarely smooth, easy-walking affairs. Parts of the concrete paving stones will have subsided or lifted; metal bars of unknown origin or use will protrude from the sidewalk, and always at angles and heights designed to geld any unwary male pedestrian and ruin his chances of producing offspring. Then there are the concrete drainage covers that may have cracked or been broken, caving into the drain and exposing an area large enough to swallow an unwary leg or baby elephant.

'Public' toilets also abound in Bangkok and its environs. Now, before those who know that in reality Bangkok suffers from a distinct lack of public urinal facilities, let me say the 'public toilets' I refer to are for men only and are exactly that, very public. As long as you are in a position to point Percy away from too many prying eyes and in the direction of foliage or a swampy area, then you can do as the motorcycle taxi boys and the pushcart food sellers do and take a 'rest stop' practically anywhere.

***

I once stayed with a girl named Apple at her mother's place in Bangkok. The house was set on a large plot of ground, alongside a pathway set back from one of Bangkok's *khlongs*. The *khlong* was heavily polluted. It had one colour, black, and was a carrier of the waste and garbage of many households. I watched as plastic bottles and containers, garbage bags and sundry discarded food items slowly floated past. Quite a bit became wedged at the edges of the *khlong* and wouldn't go any further. The remainder no doubt eventually found its way into the Chao Phrya River and thence into the Gulf of Thailand.

The houses set right on the canal were subject to the foul odour drifting up from the stagnant and polluted water. I was pleased Apple's place was one block away from the water.

The main building was a wooden two-storey construction with the usual corrugated iron roofing, making upstairs almost unbearably hot during the heat of the day. The wooden floorboards felt good under the feet and the area was very basic, consisting of only two rooms. One served as a bedroom. The other room had the main bed partitioned off from the rest by a rack of clothes on one side and wooden shelves behind. A mosquito net, a common enough sight in Thai homes, covered the main bed. The pervasive television set was placed just outside the door of the second bedroom.

Behind the television, in an alcove-like area, was the ubiquitous Buddhist altar. In a far corner were pictures of the current King and Queen of Thailand and some pictures of earlier monarchs. Further to the right of these pictures were photographs of family members, mainly past rather than present.

Apart from the various humans living in the environs of the house, a large and motley collection of rabid-looking mongrel dogs and scrawny cats inhabited the area. There was also a rooster, although it was more heard than seen.

Downstairs consisted of an attached building housing the Thai-style bathroom and kitchen area, although most cooking and food preparation took place outside, at the bottom of the stairs. Apple and her mother usually sat cross-legged on a large piece of laminated covering preparing food. The kitchen area was used primarily, it seemed, as a back up. Behind the house was a Thai-style bathroom and a smaller dwelling occupied by another family.

Just inside the front gate was one of the biggest 'spirit houses' I had ever seen. Be-decked with the usual offerings to the Buddha and sundry spirits it was bigger than some of the humpies I had seen cluttering the approaches to Hualumphong station, the main train terminal in the city. There was also the usual style of cement 'spirit house' stuck in a corner of the property.

Although every dwelling was a separate entity, there appeared to be a strong sense of community. At one end of the pathway marking the start of the community was a postage-stamp-sized reserve, alongside the stifled *khlong*. At one end, a half-moon shaped monkey bar, painted dull blue, served as home base for a clutch of five children- including Apples' younger sister Doon- playing chasings. An unsteady wooden slippery dip was a few short metres away, and behind it were four metal seesaws. The reserve had no grass, only sand, and rubbish was strewn about the area. Despite this, the children played happily. There seemed to be more children under the age of 10 than adults in this community.

Further down the lane, in the direction of the main road, was a snooker room (more an open shed with a corrugated-iron roof) with three wooden tables where the young men would congregate to hone their skills. Nearby was a general/food store selling a few basics. Everyone knew each other and visitors were common although people still locked up whenever they left their houses.

***

If there is one common aspect of travelling through the main cities of southeast Asia, it is the abundance of cars, buses, motorbikes, and the smell of diesel fumes. It is almost a rite of passage-albeit slow and tedious- linking the people of the region.

Sure, every major city has its traffic problems. Witness the Arc de Triomphe circle in Paris at peak hour or London's Trafalgar Square. Bangkok is no different from Kuala Lumpur, Jakarta, Manila or Singapore, except it probably has the worst traffic in the region. Not an easy title to lay claim to let alone hold for so many years.

Traffic in Bangkok is a favourite topic for almost all writers on the country.

This is a place where the likes of Mister Magoo would be right at home. A place where people drive in the fashion of drunks after a good belt of the giggle sauce. While some drivers should never be allowed behind the steering wheel of anything more powerful than a go-kart, there are those in control of 16-wheelers and cement trucks who drive as if they are steering a Ferrari Testosterone, or whatever it's called, in a Formula One event at Monza.

Travelling at certain points at the right time of the day on one of Bangkok's many flyover expressways you could be excused for thinking you'd been transported into a futuristic 23rd-century cityscape, a carbon copy of a Buck

Rogers or Flash Gordon city where the bulk of the traffic makes its way, not on land, but 10 to 15 metres into the sky.

In a book published in 1959 and entitled *Land of the Lotus Eaters*, the author paraphrased comments a young expatriate made to him about the state of Bangkok's traffic. "The traffic is worse than anywhere I've ever been. Buses come at you like juggernauts. Samlors dodge under your wheels. Taxis are liable to make right-hand turns across your track and...well, everybody interprets the traffic laws as he or she sees fit...You've never seen such chaos. Fortunately, nobody can drive fast enough to kill themselves or anybody else. But in the suburbs and the country..."

In the half-century since that remark, Bangkok's traffic has become almost a tourist attraction in its own right. Amazing Thailand, Amazing Traffic. Strangely, given the nature of the '*mai pen rai*' attitude of the populace, it all seems to work really well. Accidents in the city tend to be minor affairs. On the open roads, it's a different story altogether.

Although most roads, as in Western countries, have driving lanes clearly marked, a 'lane' in Thailand could be defined as any space into which a vehicle of any size or shape might- or might not- fit and it is not uncommon to see drivers taking ingenuity into their own hands and 'creating' one, two or more, extra 'lanes'.

When the traffic isn't unbearably thick, slow moving and noisy (a rarity in daylight hours), motorbikes, cars, buses, trucks and even pedestrians are liable to come out of nowhere and from all different angles and speeds.

Drivers make right and left hand turns in front of oncoming traffic, safe in the knowledge the cars, motorbikes and buses will stop before ploughing into the offending vehicle...most of the time.

It is generally accepted that the Italians are the worst drivers in Europe, if not the world. Ever since the advent of the motor vehicle, the race that has given us Ferrari, Lamborghini, and Maserati has ruled the world in vehicular discombobulation.

The Thais, given their propensity for drinking industrial quantities of lethal rotgut disguised as whisky and then clambering aboard their two-wheeled people (and furniture) movers, aren't far behind. Indeed, one man I know describes Thailand as "Italy in the tropics".

It seems some riders, once they've ingested enough alcohol to power a small lighthouse through a Siberian winter, imagine themselves to be indestructible road warriors capable of amazing ballet-like feats aboard their Yamaha Vinos and Suzuki Smash's (the latter genuinely does have a motorbike named the 'Smash').

Unfortunately, the gap between the real and the imagined is about a large bottle or two of Mekhong whisky, whereas the pliability of the average concrete telegraph pole remains constant no matter what the weather conditions or the time of day or night.

***

Taxi drivers have been negotiating the streets of the cities for so long they seem to think they are indestructible. The problem is the rest of the driving population feel they too are indestructible. Almost everyone drives around with an image of the Buddha in his or her vehicle, believing it guarantees protection from vehicular disaster.

One taxi I travelled in had no less than 13 stickers of varying types and sizes attached to the windscreen. I don't know whether they were placed so people couldn't look in or he couldn't look out. I hoped it was the former rather than the latter.

While fully aware of this propensity to vehicular insanity, I continue to put my well-being into the hands of taxi drivers on a regular basis, and have managed to remain unscathed, so far. However, one experience in particular was, to say the least, somewhat harrowing.

I was returning to Australia and shared a taxi from Pattaya to Don Muang airport with an English friend who was going back to England on a later flight. The driver we christened with the epithet 'Mad Max' for reasons that shall become clear.

He only knew two speeds: fast and faster. He overtook other vehicles with very little room to spare, aimed straight at on-coming traffic, flashed his lights and hammered his horn at anything in his way and squeezed between gaps in the traffic like a champion jockey angling for a winning run. At one point in Bangkok he reached a speed of 150 kilometres an hour on the expressway while veering in and out of lanes in the manner of a reincarnated Fangio.

'Mad Max' had the disturbing habit of dialling friends on his mobile phone while guiding his four-wheeled missile with only his right elbow. Needless to say, his speed did not drop one kilometre as he engaged in animated conversation with his countless telephone buddies.

Even worse, he was disposed to a nervous tick that involved quick flicks of his head as if he was trying to clear what may have been left of his brain.

We stopped at a petrol station for 'Mad Max' to fill his dilapidated metallic monster with more rocket fuel. My friend purchased a bottle of Lipovitan, giving it to 'Mad Max' in the hope he would slow down. Fat chance. He proceeded to drive even faster.

We made it, unscathed, to the airport in new Bangkok record time and were able to settle our nerves and our stomachs at the airport cafeteria.

***

Bangkok may be the reigning monarch, but Pattaya traffic has descended into an almost carbon-copy chaos.

Sukhumvit Highway is the main thoroughfare between Bangkok and Pattaya and as such takes a large volume of traffic. Trying to cross this highway at night can be a lengthy and precarious exercise. On one occasion, I was the pillion passenger behind a girlfriend named Da, who was going to see her school-friend Fon who lived on the other side of the highway. When we reached the highway from Central Road, Da rode along the inside of the road going against the on-coming traffic (hardly an unusual sight) until we came opposite the intersection she was hoping to enter. We sat there with a couple of other motorbikes and waited for a seeming eternity for a gap to appear in the traffic on our side. When a slight break did finally present itself, Da gunned the bike and we scooted to the centre of the highway, joining a larger collection of motorbikes and cars already waiting to cross to the other side. Finally, another break came on the other side and most of the banked-up traffic roared off into the side street.

The procedure had to be repeated on the way back an hour or so later. Getting to the centre, we waited in a group consisting of about 10 motorbikes, one car and a bus, all spewing forth a cancer-inducing concoction of gasoline and diesel fumes. After two or three minutes the bus, being the largest of our little collection, edged its way into the oncoming outside lane, forcing the traffic to stop. The car and then all the motorbikes slowly eased their way out underneath the lee of the bus until, with a rising crescendo, everybody took off as if as one.

Cockroach Soup and Purloined Bags

It was one of those days when you know you should never have got out of bed- but unfortunately it was my last day and I had a plane to catch, so I didn't have any choice.

It started with cockroaches in the chicken soup. My *mia chow* Anne and I went for breakfast and after ordering chicken soup, she received more than she bargained for, with a collection of cooked cockroaches floating along the surface. They cooked a new soup but she couldn't eat it for thinking about the other one. I couldn't really blame her. I was surprised they didn't charge extra for the cockroaches.

After breakfast, I went to visit friends in Cheena House, dropping my bags off inside the door of the foyer. Anne went for a haircut while I went upstairs to see my friends. Anne joined us later.

At 12:30 p.m., I came downstairs to take a taxi to the airport. My bags had disappeared.

A couple of Arabs had checked out and left in a baht bus, or on a pair of motorbikes, depending on who told the story and with them had gone their bags, and mine.

After my initial shock, I asked one of the motorbike taxi guys to take me to the place he'd taken the Arabs. We raced into south Pattaya and found a hotel, but they said the person I was looking for had only come to pick up a friend and had left. We then went to another hotel but drew a blank.

We returned to Cheena House but Anne had gone. The motorbike riders told me she had gone on another bike to search for the bags. I took a different motorbike taxi and went south again to scour the hotels of the Arab quarter, again without success.

We returned to *Soi* Skaw Beach Road and, as it was now 1:30 p.m. and my flight was at 5:10 p.m., I knew I would have to leave if I was to catch it.

Like most of his ilk, my taxi driver was a smoker, so we took off with the windows down while he dragged on a fag.

It wasn't long into the drive to Bangkok when the temperature gauge in his car started to show the radiator running hot, so we stopped while he put water into its hissing mouth. After about six or seven minutes we were on our way but he was forced to stop on a further two occasions to cool his steaming radiator. Each stop took up eight or 10 minutes, all precious travelling time. In order to make up time he was compelled to drive as fast as possible on the toll-ways. He was fine: he was equipped with a seatbelt; no such luxury for me. I kept imagining his clapped-out Corolla would run up the backside of the vehicle in front and I'd end up wearing the windscreen.

We managed to make it to the terminal at 4:40 p.m., just 30 minutes before scheduled take off.

I raced to the counter, checked myself in and then sought to leave details about my lost/stolen baggage. The customer service girl at British Airways was very helpful.

When it came to paying the-then 250 baht passenger service charge I ran into some problems. One booth was unmanned; a second was closed with the operator counting cash and the vending machines would only issue change for 500 baht notes. I only had 1,000 baht notes. The only operational booth had a small queue but the Japanese girl at its head was purchasing what appeared to be 50 tickets, and all separately. It was now 10 minutes before the scheduled takeoff.

Fortunately, a uniformed lady came over and, after taking care of the people in front of me- who didn't have the money in Thai baht for the tickets- she took 1,000 baht from me, obtained two 500 baht notes and put one through the machine. Eight minutes to takeoff.

I joined a small queue at Immigration and Passport Control but was waved forward by an official and whisked through the checkpoint. How they knew I was the poor desperate on his way home baggage-less after six weeks in country I don't know. Maybe they're trained to look for the bedraggled and refugee-like. Six minutes to takeoff.

I checked the appropriate gate for my flight and walked hurriedly in its direction. I managed to board the aircraft with, officially, three minutes to spare.

On the plane, I found my allotted seat occupied (the airline had doubled up) but spotted a spare seat at the very rear of the plane- next to the toilets in what is termed 'Siberia' in the restaurant trade. My seat had a broken left armrest and refused point blank to recline. It really wasn't my day.

I received a message a few days later in Australia telling me my bags had been returned intact to Cheena House. The baht bus driver (they had not gone by motorbike after all) had accidentally placed them aboard his vehicle and taken them to the local bus station. The Arabs told the driver the bags were not theirs and the driver had the decency to return them.

The Ugly Australians

7:30 p.m., Sunday, 5 November 2000 and Channel Nine in Australia put to air *60 Minutes*, its flagship and high-rating current affairs program. The lead story that night was headed, 'The Ugly Australians' with the subtitle 'men behaving badly'. It purported to feature the lives and loves of three Australian men on holiday in Pattaya. I was one of those men.

For some peculiar reason Pattaya was the focus of a great deal of overseas media attention during 2000, the bulk poorly researched, grossly inaccurate, sensationalist, insensitive, and puerile. Much of it bordered on xenophobia.

In March 2000, the American soft-porn magazine *Maxim* published an article claiming Pattaya was one of the most dangerous places on the planet. The front cover exclaimed 'Naked by Noon, Dead by Dawn, Up All Night in the World's Riskiest Beach Resort'.

Pullouts such as, 'Pattaya is a human roach motel, they check in but they don't check out' and photo captions reading, 'In Pattaya, there are two kinds of women...' and ' a blackjack can easily crack the skull' were attempts to bulwark a spurious argument and provide evidence of moral degradation. The reality that Pattaya is probably one of the safest places in the world in which to live wouldn't help sell magazines of course.

Then *Australian Penthouse*, a hard-core porn magazine, went in to bat with an equally ridiculous waste of precious trees and natural resources. The first paragraph read, in part, 'As the popular T-shirt, straining around the gut of so many tourists says: "Welcome to Pattaya, the Disneyland for Grown-ups"....' No one I know has ever seen this fabled T-shirt and, if it does exist, it certainly isn't 'popular'.

There were a number of other ridiculous statements, one being 'Hardly anyone has a suntan.' Obviously, the reporter never made it down to Jomtien or Wongamat Beaches or even strolled along the Pattaya Bay promenade during daylight hours and saw the large numbers of people out enjoying the sunshine.

After the print media, television also chimed in with a couple of lurid programs by the BBC and Channel Four in Britain during what must have been a slow period for the usual 'vicar elopes with lorry-driver' and 'naked MP in bed with choir boy' stories.

Then, early in July, I received an e-mail from Julian Cress (the son of the Archibald Prize-winning artist Fred Cress), a long-time producer with the Australian current affairs program *60 Minutes* and someone I had known for over six years.

Julian wrote *60 Minutes* was considering doing a story on Pattaya, based on the article in *Australian Penthouse*.

I immediately e-mailed him back and included my mobile number. Minutes later, he was on the phone. The wonders of modern technology.

From the outset, I told Julian if *60 Minutes* was coming to Pattaya with the aim of portraying the city as nothing more than a sexual cesspit then I wasn't interested in participating. He assured me *60 Minutes* was simply looking for the truth; tell the story and the reality of Pattaya would be self-evident.

Hindsight is a wonderful thing, and had I known what was in store, both on a personal level and for the already tarnished image of Pattaya, I would have refused any and all assistance.

Julian said he foresaw my role as bringing balance to the piece, filling in the cultural gaps that would more than likely be missing from the other interviewees. I believed if I didn't participate, the end result would likely be a complete travesty. I mistakenly felt Julian and *60 Minutes* could be trusted to do the right thing.

I have since realised a genuine expose of the scene here would merely encourage a vast increase in tourism to Thailand, and Pattaya in particular.

I didn't want to be on camera and asked Julian to supply a list of the questions I was going to be asked beforehand, so I could make sure my answers would cover all relevant points. He agreed, but as I found out later, Jeff McMullen, the presenter he generally worked with, never used a pre-arranged question format.

Julian immediately employed me as a 'fixer', the person with local knowledge who can save them wasting time and money by organising introductions to potential interviewees as well as businesspeople and the like.

Between July and September I spoke to most of the Aussie bar owners I knew, as well as a few others I thought might make good interviewees, whether on or off camera. Almost as one they expressed concern about *60 Minutes*. They believed, based on bitter past experience, any form of media coverage would be just another cheap shot at Thailand and Pattaya.

Julian maintained contact by telephone during this period and in the early stages asked if there were many Australian tourists in town, as he was looking for a more personalised angle to the story.

At the time there were very few in town, although a group of 50 Australian Rules players were supposed to be coming in early October. Julian decided they might prove to be the perfect subjects for the story.

***

Julian duly arrived, by himself, on the night of 10 October, carrying with him enough equipment to outfit a major Hollywood epic. I met him at the airport and we stayed the night in Bangkok, taking in Soi Cowboy and the infamous Thermae's Coffee Shop.

The following afternoon, we travelled by limousine down to Pattaya but that night we learned the Australian Rules players had cancelled their trip at the last minute. Maybe they knew something I didn't.

We spent the next couple of days talking with some of the bar owners while Julian shot stock footage of Pattaya, both during the day and at night, on a portable video camera, the kind used by every Japanese tourist worth his salt. He and I were unable to find anyone suitable, or willing, to participate as interviewees.

By 7:30 p.m. on Friday the 13th (lucky for some, unlucky for others so it is said), Julian was in the unenviable position of returning to Australia without a story. He said everything he had achieved to that point was, "ancillary without a couple of subjects to hang the story around."

As it happened, at the eleventh hour I found out about a couple of Australians who sounded like perfect subjects. I obtained a telephone number but it took six attempts at ringing them before we were able to make contact. They agreed to meet us at 11:00 p.m. in a place called the Moonshine Bar in *Soi* Diamond.

On the way to the bar, Julian told me not to say he was from *60 Minutes*. The warning bells should have gone off, but they didn't and it certainly wasn't alcohol stopping them.

"I'll tell them I'm an independent producer, making a documentary on Pattaya. If they ask me what program it's likely to appear on, I'll tell them it'll probably be *60 Minutes*," he said.

The two men, Mark Winter and Angus Greer, turned up with a couple of girls from a local bar. They could be best described in the Australian vernacular as 'knockabout' characters, taking life with both hands and embracing it, working and playing hard.

Mark claimed to have been a publican in Sydney and one of the people responsible for introducing Quiz and Trivia Nights into the bars of the Harbour City. He was, as we were to find out, an accomplished sailor.

Angus was in business for himself, part owner of a bar in Canberra, the Australian capital.

In the resultant *60 Minutes* piece, Mark was given the tag of a used car salesman; I was labelled a racecourse and casino gambler. It placed us on a par with politicians and pimps in a transparent effort at polarisation.

After drinking and talking with Julian, both Mark and Angus agreed to become the subjects of the *60 Minutes* story.

Over the next few days Julian took stock footage of us enjoying ourselves in the bars as well as taking a catamaran out to Koh Larn, the main tourist island in Pattaya Bay.

On 18 October, the rest of the *60 Minutes* crew, consisting of veteran reporter Jeff McMullen, cameraman Paul Bocock and soundman David Norton-Smith, arrived.

Over the next two days they followed a similar procedure to Julian, getting stock footage as well as following us through the bars and, once again, by catamaran out to Koh Larn, with Mark at the helm. On this occasion we brought along three bargirls, two from Planet Rock for Angus and I and one, named Nok, who worked in the now-defunct Playpen and was accompanying Mark.

A day or so later, while in Playpen, Mark asked me, "I know Julian's a mate of yours, but aren't you a little worried about the direction this story will take if it's done by *60 Minutes*?"

I replied I had been concerned if the footballers were the subject of the story but, "I'm not pissing in your pocket, I reckon the story will be far better because of you guys. We've got footage of you in the bars having fun but also out on the boat going to the island, so people will see there's more to Pattaya than just bars. Also, the girls looked like they were having fun and don't look downtrodden and unhappy. I think that's important. With the footballers it would have been all drinking and bars, whereas this I think will flesh out the real Pattaya."

What I hadn't banked on was Jeff McMullen's biased voiceover, an equally slanted interview with well-known Senator Mechai Viravaidya, and creative editing of the film footage.

If my warning antenna had been switched on from the outset, I should have been able to see the end result would not be in keeping with Julian's early telephone assurances.

He knew he would be working with Jeff McMullen and my request for a list of questions prior to my interview was not viable or likely. He hadn't wanted people to know he was working for *60 Minutes*, preferring that they think he was doing a documentary on Pattaya. After returning to Australia, he telephoned me on the Friday before the program went to air, promising to call back on the Monday after the show. He never rang. He also sent an e-mail on 9 November, promising to send me a copy of the tapes, including all unedited material. It has never materialised.

***

The first inkling *60 Minutes* had done a 'hatchet' job was when I received an e-mail from a friend who wrote, 'they look as though they're going to do a number on you'.

The piece opened with a 'bouncer' (to borrow a cricketing phrase) designed to pump prime the viewing audience: 'Warning, this program contains scenes of sexual exploitation'.

If that wasn't enough to signal the 'tack' *60 Minutes* had decided to take on the story then the title, 'The Ugly Australians' certainly left no one in any doubt.

The picture accompanying the headline, 'The ugly Australians', featured myself being hugged by three Thai girls. The scene came from a bar called Pussy Galore, ironic in the sense this was the former Lightning Jack's.

Jeff McMullen began his spiel with, "While prostitution is illegal in Thailand, its sex industry is thriving...with Australian men some of the best customers."

He went on to say around 60,000 Australians visited Pattaya each year and some 80 percent of them came for sex, despite the fact prostitution has been illegal in Thailand since 1960.

"In a country where poverty forces many women into prostitution and where one in five is HIV positive, these men brag about multiple partners and unprotected intercourse," he continued.

The reality is because of poverty some women choose to go into prostitution and, according to unsubstantiated sources, one in five is allegedly HIV positive.

The girls working in the sex industry in Pattaya do so of their own volition. They could choose to remain on upcountry farms and villages eking out a subsistence living, but choose to come to the bright lights and engage in sex for money with foreign men. They could just as easily choose to work in Thai brothels, where the majority of girls who work in the sex trade wind up, and where the rate of HIV infection is allegedly extremely high.

No one goes upcountry into the villages and *forces* available girls to come to Pattaya. There are plenty who come here and dislike the whole scene so much they turn around and go back from whence they came. The option is there; they're not bought and sold.

‘Collecting the evidence’: Soundman David Norton-Smith and cameraman Paul Bocock train their equipment on a prostrate Angus while the two Thai girls chat about important matters, such as the gastronomic delights of Issan cuisine.

Many girls marry foreigners and are thus removed from the industry. Others, more street smart, avoid marriage and merely take as many boyfriends as possible, extracting as much money as they can from them.

McMullen continued drawing the battle lines: “Indeed, they brag about a lot: the booze, the sex and their (paid for) conquests. They have little shame. But they’re shaming Australia and, in the process, risking death by AIDS.”

In my own case, I’m a purely social drinker. Julian, on the other hand, certainly managed to consume large quantities of expense-account beer during his two-week stay in Bangkok and Pattaya.

Additionally, as Julian was aware, I had two girlfriends at the time, both had never worked in the sex industry and I did not pay them for their sexual favours. One had been living with me for the previous 16 months.

As for the ‘bragging’, it appears a reporter asking a question about sexual activity and receiving an answer constitutes ‘bragging’. All three of us were asked by McMullen how many women we thought we’d been sexually involved with in Thailand. We all gave different, allegedly ‘bragging’, answers.

As regards us ‘shaming Australia’, does this mean men having sex with women who are prostitutes, sex workers, bargirls or whatever in any country other than Australia are guilty of ‘shaming’ our beautiful homeland? The implication of that statement I believe borders on racism and xenophobia.

It is well known that the greatest concentration of ‘working girls’ is to be found in the great ports of the world. Why? Because sailors who have been at sea for extended periods are perfect targets for sex workers the world over.

Yet the sailors of Australia, who ply the sea-lanes of the world, are not vilified by *60 Minutes*. Nobody accuses them of ‘shaming’ Australia. Are the airline pilots and stewards who have stopovers in various cities around the globe and indulge in sex with local women 'shaming' Australia?

If anything the *60 Minutes* crew perpetrated one of the best scenes of sexual exploitation in the program. Towards the end of the piece Nok, Mark's new 19-year-old girlfriend, without the cameras on her, pulled aside her bikini top to bare her breasts. Anyone can witness this sight on almost any beach in Australia and in many other places around the world. What viewers weren't told was she'd already done it a few seconds before and Paul Bocock, the cameraman, said, "I didn't get that, could she do it again?"

So, Nok, having done it the first time merely for fun, was pressured by the *60 Minutes* crew to again bare her breasts, this time for the camera. Just who was exploiting whom?

Equally exploitative was a short piece of footage shot by Julian about a 69-year-old Australian man from Queensland who was enjoying himself with a girl from Pussy Galore. Certainly she was young enough to his granddaughter, but he was a regular customer in the bar and friendly with the girls. They liked and respected him. *60 Minutes* decided to 'put the boot in' when, after initially agreeing to go on camera and be interviewed, he later declined. Nevertheless, Julian had garnered sufficient information about him to use as a cameo piece in the story. With Angus, Mark, and myself he at least had three willing participants, the Queenslander he simply bushwhacked.

As for myself, there was no mention I was on the *60 Minutes* payroll as a 'fixer'. Nor was there any mention of the fact I had learnt enough Thai- albeit at a rudimentary level- to be enable Julian and the crew to travel wherever they wanted to go. There was no mention I was a journalist who had written a book on southeast Asian history.

Indeed, when we were first introduced Jeff McMullen told me he had read an article I had written for an Internet site about prostitution in Thailand, finding it "informative".

***

In a strange twist of fate, Jeff McMullen was sacked from *60 Minutes* eight days after 'The Ugly Australians' story went to air. He had been with the program for 16 years.

McMullen's Machiavellian nature was revealed within a day or two of his removal as he went into damage control regarding his reputation. According to the front page of the *Sydney Morning Herald* newspaper of 14 November, McMullen had the temerity to blame his sacking on his 'continual complaints about the show's cheque-book journalism and tabloidism...'

He was quoted as saying the Nine Network and *60 Minutes* had '...lost sight that it is credibility, truth and honour of the program that drive viewers to it in the beginning.'

At one point during his sojourn in Pattaya, McMullen told me John Westacott, the Executive Producer of *60 Minutes* was, "a dickhead who doesn't care about the story so much as whether it rates." Yet, this is the same man who, when asked by Angus if *60 Minutes* was going to "stitch us up," replied earnestly, "No mate, we are just looking for the truth." But the truth from what standpoint? Clearly, one based around sensationalism, tabloidism and an obsession with ratings.

I was amazed McMullen had the audacity to try and claim the moral high ground for himself after putting to air a piece he knew was a travesty of the truth designed to propagate a populist viewpoint. At no point while he was here did he verbally express his 'shock' and 'disgust' (two words he used in his preamble), keeping his true feelings and intentions to himself.

From right to left: Jeff McMullen, Julian Cress, cameraman Paul Bocock and Nok, in the background.

'Interrogating' the offenders: Julian Cress and Jeff McMullen chat amiably with Mark Winter.

On the *60 Minutes* section of the ninemsn.com.au website, Internet browsers were asked to respond to a couple of inflammatory questions.

The first was, 'Do these men make you feel ashamed to be Australian?'

As every pollster worth his salt knows, a question can be framed to elicit a particular response, be it either 'Yes' or 'No'. In this case, the question was so obviously loaded as to be almost ridiculous.

Naturally, the majority of people were going to vote 'Yes' and by the end of the voting period 3,216 people had voted in the affirmative as opposed to 1,391 who voted 'No'.

The second question, 'Should the Thai or Australian Governments be doing more to enforce safer sex practices?' brought 489 responses. Those who hoped we would catch AIDS, or castrated or flogged, made up around 56 percent, while those who were either neutral or even supportive amounted to about 44 percent. When broken down by gender, the figures, not surprisingly, showed 86 percent of female respondents heavily against us.

Julian witnessed the girls in operation in Pattaya and was even a target for one, an 18-year-old girl named Puay who tried ever so hard to get him to sleep with her. However, he seemed to have expunged Puay and her machinations from his memory bank because that would conflict with the 'forced into prostitution' and 'sexual exploitation' stance of the program. Many other girls couldn't understand why he didn't take a girl to his room, even though he explained he had a girlfriend back in Australia.

In my lengthy on-camera interview with Jeff McMullen, I pointed out some of the cultural differences and attitudes to sex between Thailand and most Western nations. None of my statements saw the light of day.

In fact, the highly-respected Senator Mechai Viravaidya represented the 'home side'. Appointed as

Thailand's UN AIDS ambassador, Mechai, to his credit, almost single-handedly promoted the use of condoms among sex workers and the general population throughout the country.

When interviewed by *60 Minutes* he claimed one in five of the working girls of Pattaya are HIV positive. To the best of my knowledge, there are no reliable figures to back up his assertion.

He labelled the foreign men who come to Pattaya as 'predators'. The understandable reality is that Thai men, in general, dislike foreigners. I can't really blame them. We come over here with more money than the average Thai and can throw it around and attract the women. If the roles were reversed and Thai men were coming to Australia for 'cheap' sex, Australian men would be indignant.

It was interesting how no mention was made that the majority of Thai girls, particularly those dancing in the go-go bars, had Thai boyfriends and husbands. The numbers of *meng da* (pimps) who live off the earnings of their girlfriends is quite high, so just who are the real 'predators'?

Christopher Moore, a Canadian novelist and former university professor living in Thailand, stated in an interview with the Bangkok-based *The Big Chilli* magazine, '...It is nearly impossible to generalize about the sex worker or the customer. There is great comfort in such generalizations but comfort is an illusion as the reality is always often far more noble and far more sordid and terrible. In other words, what goes on in the night world of Bangkok [read Pattaya] is filled with contradictions. The Thais are far cleverer than the *farang* as they are content to live with ambiguity; it is the foreigners who go mad trying to resolve what cannot be resolved. That good and evil, wrong and right, honesty and dishonesty, betrayal and loyalty are mostly blurred, that life rarely renders a clear-cut definition between the extremes and we spend most of our time in the grey areas...We live in an age of Hollywood where complexity is greeted with horror- simple answers, simple images.'

***

The fallout from the program continued in one form or another for some time. Over the course of the next 18 months or so, a large number of people recognised me and chatted about the program. I was surprised because I certainly wouldn't remember a particular face from a 15-minute one-off television program. Reactions varied from "How did you let *60 Minutes* stitch you up?" to "I thought it was an OK piece." One person, who approached me in Giligin's, a go-go bar in Pattayaland Soi 1, has since become a friend while another, who spoke to me in the coffee shop of the Honey Hotel in Bangkok, a week after the program went to air, presented me with a bottle of Jacob's Creek red wine.

Angus Greer, after returning to Canberra for a few months, came back to Pattaya and started seeing a dancer from Playpen on a regular basis. They eventually moved in together, married, and had a child.

Mark Winter continued to see Nok and he purchased a beer bar in Soi Chaiyapoom. It soon became apparent Mark was not the wealthy retiree he claimed to be. In fact, he was more Walter Mitty than Gordon Gecko. As the bar failed to attract custom, he borrowed money from friends and acquaintances. The bar soon closed and Mark disappeared.

In early 2002, I received an e-mail from Mark telling me he was in Australia and been in contact with the *Courier Mail* newspaper in Brisbane. Apparently they were interested in his story as yet another example of cheque-book journalism. They wanted to know whether *60 Minutes* bought drinks for girls in the bars as well paid the bar fines for the dancers we took to Koh Larn. Jeff McMullen had won a settlement against Channel Nine in the NSW Industrial Relations Court and the issue of cheque-book journalism in relation to *60 Minutes* had raised its head. Mark believed it was a good time to strike, although he was more interested in how much money he might be able to squeeze out of Channel Nine.

Chris Griffith, a journalist with the *Courier Mail* contacted me and said the newspaper had asked *60 Minutes* about Mark's allegations. Their reply came via a letter from lawyers for Channel Nine. According to Chris, in the letter *60 Minutes* stated at no time had the crew acted improperly by paying for us to be with bargirls and, secondly, Julian alleged he only met me briefly at a party some years before. This was a foolish and easily exposed lie.

On 16 October, Julian had 'rung the bell' in Playpen. This meant *60 Minutes* purchased a round of drinks for everybody present in the bar at the time. The bill came to more than 1,000 baht.

On 19 October, Julian and- by extension- *60 Minutes,* paid the 500 baht bar fines in Planet Rock for the girls Angus and I were to take to Koh Larn island the next day. They also paid for two rooms at the Flamingo Hotel (a total of around 700 baht) so we could spend the night with these girls. He also paid for Nok's bar fine in Playpen.

My own records showed I first met Julian in July 1994 when he, his girlfriend Megan Brownlow, and I had dinner at an Indonesian restaurant in Newtown. From mid-1989 until 1991 I had spent time doing radio shows at 2RPH in Sydney. It was here I met Megan and we became friends. She later started working at 2UE as a producer for Gary O'Callaghan and later John Laws. We maintained contact over the years and this led to my meeting Julian.

In April 1997, I attended Julian's birthday party at the house he shared with Megan in Newtown, and in June the same year went to a Variety Club fundraiser with them, held in the Newtown Hotel. The night before I returned to Thailand in October 2000, I spent as a guest (the fatted calf perhaps) in their house.

The story never ran in the *Courier Mail.* In early March, I received another e-mail from Mark claiming Frank Brewer QC, a leading Queensland barrister, was prepared to act for him against Channel Nine. He had advised Mark to prevent any newspaper article going to print. To the best of my knowledge, the case never reached a court or a settlement.

***

What surprised me most about the *60 Minutes* piece was I believed Julian and Jeff McMullen understood, at least in a cursory way, the nature of the Pattaya prostitution paradigm. It seemed as though once they were safely ensconced in Australia all they learned about Pattaya was discarded in favour of the more populist and socially acceptable standards extant in most Western Christian-oriented countries.

I was reminded many people find it difficult to come to terms with the reality of difference. For example, the great English novelist and journalist Graham Greene once wrote, 'I have sometimes wondered whether they [critics] go round the world blinkered. "This is Indo-China," I want to exclaim, "this is Mexico, this is Sierra Leone carefully and accurately described. I have been a newspaper correspondent as well as a novelist. I assure you that the dead child lay in the ditch in just that attitude. In the canal of Phat Diem the bodies stuck out of the water..." But I know that argument is useless. They won't believe the world they haven't noticed is like that.'

The question is what are we morally outraged by? Is it that sex is relatively cheap by Western standards, and likely to be less hurried and impersonal? The money some of these girls can make in one night is far greater than they would ever expect to earn in a week, and sometimes a month, seems lost on those who condemn the people who come to Thailand and indulge in sex with women who have *chosen* to provide sexual favours to foreign men.

Are we outraged by the fact some Caucasian men prefer the company- albeit generally superficially and largely sexually- of dark-skinned Thai and southeast Asian women? Is there a deep-rooted streak of Aryan-style elitism that makes some Westerners fear the potential dilution of the white race?

There appears to be an element of jealousy attached to much of the reporting on Pattaya and Thailand. The mendacious hacks who find their way here seem to possess a flagellant urge that would have propelled them towards canonisation in a world once dominated by the Holy Inquisition. These petty jealousies combine with their pious moralising tones to produce a fodder consumed whole and unquestioned by a pliable public grown complacent by a constant stream of media sound bites.

Perhaps the views expressed by the minions who venture into Pattaya say more about their own sexual dysfunction, and that of the publishers and producers who lap it up with such religious fervour, than the people on whom they report.

This is an advertisement that appeared in a 1970 edition of the now-defunct *Bangkok World* newspaper. The Pattaya Palace Hotel was then the pre-eminent sleeping den in the burgeoning resort town. The hotel has been un-occupied for many years, but in 2004 plans were underway to renovate and refurbish the old building and restore it to its former glory.

3

Here, There, Everywhere

Goin' Up the Country

One of my first experiences of travelling to the village or town of a girlfriend took place when I went to a place called Kra Nuan, 60 kilometres outside of the northeastern city of Khon Kaen.

Accompanying me was a 25-year-old girl named Dook. She worked at a Belgian-run bar called the Welkomm Inn (colloquially known as the Belgian Embassy) and her friend became involved with Manchester Dave while I somehow found myself with Dook.

She invited me to her home and we caught a tour bus from the Morchit Terminal in Bangkok. The bus departed at 9:30 p.m. and the hostess distributed a single 'Food Box' to each passenger. It contained a small piece of cake and a drink of either warm chocolate milk or warm orange juice; it was the luck of the draw as to which liquid you received.

The bus seats were reasonably comfortable with plenty of legroom and eased back a long way to enable sleep: that is, all except mine, which appeared to be broken, and only reclined back half-way. Adding to the discomfiture there were times when the noxious odour from the on-board toilet permeated the bus, making it smell like a sewerage outfall.

When we pulled into Khon Kaen at 4:00 a.m., we were besieged by a horde of taxi drivers looking to obtain the lucrative fare to Kra Nuan. At that time in the morning I couldn't be bothered to haggle and agreed to pay a massive 400 baht for a driver to travel to Dook's place.

Dook's family home consisted of grey concrete blocks topped with corrugated iron roofing. Internally, wooden partitions had been erected to create two bedrooms. The bathroom contained the usual squat Thai-style toilet and a concrete washbasin, left open to the elements to allow rainwater to fill it. Outside the makeshift kitchen were large earthenware jars topped with aluminium guttering, also designed to entrap rainwater. In the yard roamed the usual motley collection of malnourished dogs and the odd fowl.

The house was occupied by Dook's mother and father (away in Bangkok when we arrived), two younger sisters, one older sister, and three young children. As with so many places it looked like a bomb had gone off inside and the residents had only just cleared an area in which to sit.

The eldest sister was married to a Thai. Of the others, one was married to a Dutchman, the other to a German. Both of Dook's younger sisters had formerly worked in bars in Pattaya. Perhaps bar work was something of a family tradition. They were certainly doing a sterling job of cementing international ties. The girls married to foreigners had managed to raise the lifestyle of the whole family, thereby gaining respect for their parents in the village.

At 6:30 a.m. (yes, in the morning) the place became akin to an early opener when two large bottles of Singha beer appeared, were opened and consumed over the next hour or so by the girls and sundry inquisitive neighbours.

Two of the sisters went to the market and brought back some chicken for breakfast. Dook and her younger sister suggested I check into the only hotel in town. By motorbike, it was five minutes from their place on the road to Khon Kaen. The rooms were reasonably spacious with air-conditioning, a refrigerator and hot shower, all for 450 baht a night.

After moving into the hotel room, I returned to Dook's place and later went with her younger sister to the local food market.

Vegetable and fruit sellers abounded and sides of meat were hung up in the open air, attracting hordes of flies. Slaughtered, plucked chickens were laid out on wooden tables, also attracting their share of flies. We bought a whole chicken for just 50 baht. The flies came free.

The chicken was the chief ingredient for an excellent soup (maybe the flies gave it a special tang) and that night I took Dook and her elder sister out for dinner to the hotel coffee shop-cum-karaoke bar.

The Japanese may have lost the Second World War and won the peace, but their lingering world legacy may well be the karaoke bar. The sounds of people being slowly strangled and castrated with blunt instruments at the same time. Maybe it's just wishful thinking on my part.

This was my first experience of a country karaoke bar and the hotel had about six or seven girls of varying ages working as singers.

The next day Dook's mother returned from Bangkok and we had a lunch that consisted of me, Dook, her mother, and sisters and about 15 other men, women and children who came to see this apparition in their midst.

I checked out of the hotel the following morning and took a songthaew to the local bus station and paid 18 baht for the lengthy bus trip into Khon Kaen- a far cry from the 400 baht I'd forked out for the early morning taxi ride a few days earlier. Dook decided to stay with her family for a couple of days and I rarely saw her when she returned to Pattaya.

***

Later I met Suetat, a 25-year-old who told me she was from a little village in Buriram province, not far from the Cambodian border. Her English was good and she told me she had a four-year-old daughter (later she admitted the 'daughter' was actually her youngest sister) and had been working in Pattaya for two years.

Suetat said she had a German boyfriend she'd been seeing for about a year, spending three months at his home in Germany earlier that year. He was sending her 5,000 baht a month in an effort to stop her working in the bar. Suetat said it was not enough so she was back working. I suspect her German boyfriend was unaware she was back in the bars.

Suetat told me she left school at the age of 12 and went to Bangkok to look for work. She cleaned rooms for about two years and then went to work in a factory, making shoes, for the next six years.

Her mother had given birth to her youngest sister and was living in a run-down place not big enough for the family. Suetat knew a girl in her village who had gone to work in the bars of Pattaya and Bangkok and made enough money to build a house worth 500,000 baht and owned a car. Suetat's older 'cousin' was also working at a bar in Soi 8 in Pattaya. These 'success' stories made her decide to come to work in the bars.

Suetat said she was a virgin until she was 23 and had never been with a Thai man. A German she met in Bangkok was the first man she'd slept with.

A few days later, I accompanied Suetat and her flatmate and fellow village resident Pim, by taxi to their village in Buriram. We left Pattaya at 8:00 a.m. and the taxi driver, who spoke excellent English, told me he had worked in Saudi Arabia and Norway. Each time we passed a roadside Buddhist shrine he 'honked' the horn, I presume to wake up the spirits so they would give us good luck as we made our way along Thailand's notorious highways and byways.

Suetat's parents' house in Buriram was a large two-tiered split-level affair made of wood and corrugated iron. Upstairs was the living area, one large room with an uneven wooden floor, divided into two sleeping areas. There was a fridge Suetat had purchased a few months earlier, and the usual television set. The walls were of corrugated iron and wood and did not reach the roof, thus allowing air and mosquitoes to circulate. On a wooden pole was the central power supply, with power cords running everywhere.

Underneath the house was a raised wooden platform where much of the food preparation was done. There was also a concrete room used for storage and also for sleeping. Inside was a small generator connected to water pipes while at the rear of the property was a large pond filled with rainwater. This water supplied much of the village.

A man turned up on a motorised tractor/trailer, started the generator and filled three 44-gallon drums. There was a constant stream of people coming down the side path with large wooden wheelbarrows holding earthenware jars. They stopped at the lake and filled the jars.

Near to the dirt lane was the concrete 'bathroom', the usual Thai-style squat toilet and shower area. The house also had a side shed containing the rice surplus.

Suetat showed me a block of land she said she'd bought for 50,000 baht. She told me her German boyfriend had given her close to 100,000 baht over the previous few months to stop her working in the bar.

Speaking of her time in Germany she said, "My boyfriend used to go out drinking a lot and would leave me at home with his mother. He didn't show me much attention and I used to cry sometimes. I didn't think I could stay with him for a long time."

When we had arrived, her father, mother, and Noot, her 20-year-old sister, were out working in the rice fields. When they returned that afternoon, they seemed to be accompanied by half the neighbourhood.

It turned out the village 'telegraph' had worked overtime and they had come to see the *farang*. A special slap-up meal was prepared with the main course being snake *a la cuisine de paddy field*.

If you are going to spend any time in southeast Asia away from the comfort of resort hotels and major tourist centres then the chances are you will have to sample some of the traditional fare of the country you're visiting. In the cities and major towns of Thailand there are usually franchises of American fast food giants like McDonalds and KFC available for the wimps of the culinary department. In the small towns and villages, you have no choice but to eat Thai food or go hungry. I've learnt enough Thai to be able to ask for a few simple, yet filling, dishes. These are mainly chicken and rice meals cooked in a variety of different ways.

Even in Bangkok, in the outer suburbs especially, it can be difficult to find someone who speaks or understands any English. Therefore, learning some Thai became essential if I wished to continue to travel around by myself and eat in Thai food places.

While in Vientiane in Laos, I managed to come across a great restaurant operating out of a run-down French colonial-era mansion that served the best pepper steak I have ever tasted in my life. That the meat may have originally been the buttocks of an anti-government Hmong tribesperson rather than sliced from a cow mattered not a bit. It tasted like meat heaven.

The Buriram snake had been freshly caught and killed in the paddy fields. The meat was mince-like and gristly, like trying to consume the pebbles on a gravel driveway. I don't know if it was the particular brand of snake I was eating or whether this gristly taste is common to the slithery reptiles. Snake also happened to find its way onto the menu the following night. Nevertheless, I still draw the line at consuming grasshoppers, the feet of chickens, and live beetles. I find it quite disconcerting to think your meal is capable of wandering off the plate to reconnoitre the table.

At one stage, there were at least 25 people sitting around downstairs and most of them were getting inebriated on beer and a Thai whisky that looked like tepid water, smelt like methylated spirits, and tasted like cough mixture mixed in diesel fuel. It's a liquid (and I use that word in its broadest sense) popularly known as *lao khao*.

Suetat had a small white rabbit she called 'Jimmy'. She brought it with her and that night a small ginger cat and the rabbit checked each other out. The rabbit moved toward the cat and the cat backed off. Perhaps Thai cats are real wimps, or genuine Buddhists.

Early the next morning Suetat's lean father and an 86-year-old Khmer man were getting stuck into the *lao khao* for breakfast. Mind you, they were still drunk from the night before, so perhaps it was more a hair of the dog kind of thing.

Suetat told me we were going to an historic site known as Kao Phanom Rung. We boarded a covered truck and were accompanied by what seemed to be half the village. As it was, 16 people faced the starter.

Apart from me, Suetat, her mother, father, her sisters Noot and four-year-old Tam, her 21-year-old friend Mutt and her 10-month-old baby boy, the 86-year-old wizened little Khmer man, seven others also climbed aboard the truck to go to the historic site.

The old Khmer man sat next to me on the bench seat in the back of the truck, the standard Khmer red and white checked scarf wrapped about his waist. He would have been about 160 centimetres tall (five foot four inches) if he'd been able to stand to his full height; as it was, he was bent over at the waist and stood all of about 150 centimetres (four-and-a-half feet). He ate absolutely anything and everything, and drank the same. On the bus, we had some plain biscuits, and the old devil scoffed as many as he could get his gnarled hands on. The chip packets suffered the same fate.

We reached Phanom Rung, an ancient Khmer temple situated on top of an extinct volcano with commanding views of the surrounding plains. The place had been restored from a pile of stones to something like its former glory.

Our bus apparently didn't have the 'strength' to cart 16 people up the steep road to the entrance of Phanom Rung so we hitched a ride in the back of a pick-up truck.

The old boy wandered about munching whatever food and taking as much drink (preferably alcoholic) as he could while ruminating loudly. Suetat told me he had a daughter who had gone to Sweden four years earlier and he hadn't heard from her since. The girl had previously had a baby to a Chinese man and dealt in heroin. Chances are she had come to an untimely demise.

Later I walked across the road and found something to eat. I looked across the road and saw the old boy squatting and- you guessed it- filling his face yet again.

After returning to the village, I decided to take a walk around. You could almost touch and smell the poverty and the tough lives most of these people were leading. The roads were dusty unsealed tracks, the houses mainly wood and corrugated iron structures, some raised a few feet off the ground, some higher, to keep snakes out and allow air to circulate underneath. It also allowed clothes to dry out of the rain.

It was around 5:00 p.m. and the farmers were coming home, herding their primary asset or assets, namely two, three or four water buffalo.

That night I also met the only other foreigner in the village. His name was Hans but everybody called him 'Poo', an unfortunate cognomen for which I never learned the origin. He was a Dutchman and stayed with his girlfriend Sa whenever he came to Thailand. He said Khmer Rouge soldiers had wandered into the town the previous New Year's Eve; Cambodia was only a couple of kilometres away and the-then Khmer Rouge stronghold was nearby. In fact, Khmer was the language of choice in the village rather than Thai.

Sa's house was set on a large piece of land and cost 100,000 baht to build. It was a solid and imposing brick structure with blue-tiled floors, ceiling fans and plenty of rooms- all made possible courtesy of Sa's forays into the world of prostitution. She had been the inspiration for Suetat's move to Pattaya.

Suetat claimed her mother had only 48 baht in the bank and she realised she was going to have to help her youngest sister, Tam. She also said her mother and father had never gone to school and, consequently, could not read or write. Her parents worked in the rice paddies for about 110 baht a day.

She said her younger brother Tok was coming second in his class (out of 50 students) at school and she wanted him to continue for as long as possible. She knew the value of a good education in the race for the best jobs.

"My father never used to work, but now he have to because my family need money," she told me.

She said the house we stayed in cost about 10,000 baht to build, but before that her parents had lived in a much smaller place and her mother couldn't sleep because of the rain. Suetat was desperate to take care of her mother.

"Sometimes I wish I was dead. I have to take care of my family and I think too much." Only her sister Noot knew what she did, although she thought her mother suspected.

No wonder so many girls leave the villages in search of greater wealth. Boredom is another reason why the bright lights of Bangkok and Pattaya also beckon. Everyday in the village is a little like the movie *Groundhog Day*. Get up, eat, sort of work or wander about and visit, sleep, eat, watch television, eat, nap, eat, sleep.

I am constantly amazed at the ability of the Thais to sleep almost anywhere and at anytime and on surfaces not designed for the contours of the human form. I have seen motorbike taxi boys fast asleep while sprawled across their machines at unnatural angles, while not a few metres away, a radio will be blaring out music at deafening decibels.

While I was in Suetat's village, the annual festival of Loy Krathong took place. Along with Songkran, it is the biggest celebration of the Thai year. For a day or two before the festival, the girls of the village were busy making little boats, called *krathong*, out of banana leaves and putting candles on them. The festival is an offering to the gods of rainmaking and at night, the *krathong* candles are lit and floated on the water.

Back at home, Suetat's father had been busy plucking a scrawny, old-aged, freshly slaughtered chicken and was starting to broil it over a small open fire. We had eel, frankfurts, and chicken for dinner. The meat on the recently deceased chicken proved as impervious as the old bird.

In the dark of the early evening, while we ate by the light of a single bulb and the village was in almost total darkness the peace was broken by rock and roll Thai music emanating at close to full volume from next door.

The following morning the quiet tranquillity of the village was broken at 6:30 a.m. by a cacophony of sound: the neighbours with the stereo turned up full blast and visitors to Suetat's place talking in loud voices. Forget any thoughts of sleep.

I went downstairs later and sat around a new tiled table Suetat had bought for the family. Also sat at the table were two or three wizened old ladies with betel-stained teeth. Papa, a good-natured old soul even though he was drunk most of the time, sat with them along with a younger man.

All of a sudden, a fistfight broke out between two of the old crones. Suetat's mother and father eventually broke it up but one old lady went home with bruises while the other lost a decent clump of hair.

Later that day, Suetat, her mother, young sister and Tam, and I walked some five or six kilometres to the next village by way of rice paddy berms and red clay lanes to watch Loy Krathong festivities at the local school. Suetat told me her brother Tok walked this distance to and from school every day.

After watching a motley collection of people bedecked in multi-coloured clothing march around the sports field we went down to a small shop on the main street and watched the passing parade. The odd *katoey* dressed in 'her' krathong finest; young children dressed in similar fashion, Loy Krathong queens sitting atop motor vehicles festooned with flowers and cushions. Young and not so young Thai men walked the street drinking whisky and getting louder. It was a bit like a football crowd but without the aura of violence.

In the late afternoon we stopped at Pim's place and I gained a first-hand feeling of how a monkey feels in a zoo. While we ate watermelon, an old crone wandered across the dirt road and squatted not two metres from me. She remained silent while smiling at me through betel-stained teeth.

We returned to Pattaya the next day. A couple of months later Suetat's German boyfriend came back, took her to Bangkok and Phuket, married her, and they returned to Germany.

Travel All Over the Countryside

One of the best ways of seeing the countryside is via the railway. Railways extend for just over 4,000 kilometres around the country and my first experience of rail travel took place after I had ventured by tour bus west of Bangkok to the city and province of Kanchanaburi.

I stayed at a bungalow complex consisting of about eight separate rooms, all with internal bathrooms and air-conditioning units that, in my room at least, sounded like a Harrier jump jet ready for take-off.

Kanchanaburi was a typical town: flags wherever there was a spare pole; plenty of motorcyclists careening down the streets at ridiculous speeds; whitewashed concrete building monstrosities; uneven sidewalks; a multitude of street food stalls selling every type of food imaginable. Being the cultural Neanderthal I am, I had KFC (yes, it's even here in the provinces) the next morning for breakfast.

Kanchanaburi is a place of great beauty tarnished by a spectre of evil that took place during the Second World War. For it was here the infamous bridge over the River Kwai was constructed as part of the Burma-Siam railway.

The Japanese, having occupied Malaya, Singapore, and most of Burma, and with Thailand as an ally, decided to construct a single-gauge railway from Malaya to Burma to carry troops and supplies.

In the hot, humid, malarial jungle surrounding Kanchanaburi, the brave knights of Bushido practised their unique brand of Japanese chivalry on Australian, British and Dutch prisoners of war as well as impressed labour from Malaya and Thailand. So many people died in its construction the track is known as the 'Death Railway'.

In Kanchanaburi, there are two main war cemeteries. At Chung Kai, the site of a base camp, the cemetery contains the graves of 1,740 British and Dutch prisoners of war while the main Kanchanaburi cemetery holds the 1,362 Australians who died while working to further the glory of the Japanese empire. It also holds the graves of other British and Dutch soldiers not interred at Chung Kai.

The bridge over the River Kwai is not the original wooden structure, but a refurbished version of the second bridge thrown over the river by the prisoners of war. The bridge was not constructed by Alec Guinness and blown up by William Holden, but during a raid by Allied bombers.

Nowadays you can traverse the bridge by way of narrow wooden planks. In what is a scenic setting it is hard to imagine the untold suffering that went into its construction.

I left Kanchanaburi by an open-window, feel-the-breeze, ceiling fan bus and went to the town of Ratchaburi. One good thing about the local bus system is that although there are designated bus stops it is possible to just stand by the side of the road and flag one down. If you want to get off the bus, you merely walk to the front of the vehicle and say when.

Rail travel is classified into three grades: express, fast and ordinary. In Thailand, this means slow, slower and slowest. Nevertheless, it is one of the best and most exciting ways of seeing the countryside.

The 3:30 p.m. train to Hat Yai arrived at 4:00 p.m., just as the afternoon monsoon decided to dump its 30 centimetres of water on Ratchaburi.

I made the mistake of travelling Third Class (overnight) from Ratchaburi to Hat Yai, in the south of Thailand. Third Class means bench seats hewn from the instruments of torture used by the Spanish Inquisition and are barely wide enough for two people to sit on; smokers and non-smokers travel as one; and there is no reserved seating, just first come, first serve. The bench seats are bearable for about four hours, but once night falls and the brain starts to get foggy they become quite uncomfortable.

The train stops at nearly every station on the run down to Hat Yai. At most stations are an assembled multitude of merchants attempting to sell rice dinners, soups, sweets, pineapples, bananas, mangoes, coffee, Singha beer, water and (you can smell them coming) fish sticks. At Hua Hin, I purchased a warm- not hot- sugar-laced, three-sips-and-it-was-gone, cup of coffee for 10 baht.

The motley collection of passengers in my carriage included a Buddhist monk aged anywhere from 80 to 200 years old. Awake, he coughed, spluttered and wheezed, sounding as if he would expire at any tick of the clock. However, he settled down to a fine old sleep until we reached Hua Hin. He then roused himself from his repose, lit up a bunger and proceeded to cough, splutter and wheeze yet again. After finishing the cancer stick, he thankfully returned to peaceful slumber.

The scheduled 14-hour train trip finally ended after 15 hours as we rolled into Hat Yai. I had attempted to sleep on my bench seat but found the exercise impossible. In Hat Yai, I found a hotel and spent a few hours surveying the backs of my eyelids.

Hat Yai, some 60 kilometres from the Malaysian border, is located in the predominantly Muslim provinces of the south and many women wear traditional head coverings and a large mosque is located near the train line. There is also a large Chinese merchant presence with numerous shop signs displaying both Thai and Chinese script.

The traffic is also well ordered. There were also streets patrolled by parking officers where on differing day's only cars with number plates ending in odd or even numbers could park. Of course, for a few baht, a parking officer can be 'persuaded' to become ignorant in matters of odd and even numbering.

There are also a large number of traditional, and not-so-traditional, massage parlours where a two-hour massage will cost about 200 baht. A Malaysian man who thought I was an American- even though I was wearing nothing louder than a blue T-shirt- kindly pointed me in the direction of a number of establishments.

On each of the five floors of my hotel were maids designated to attend to the rooms and at 7:30 a.m. they seemed intent- at least on my floor- on making sure further sleep was rendered difficult, if not impossible, by shouting to each other. Of course one or two may have been deaf, but in that case I would have preferred they learn sign language.

I again went Third Class by train to Surat Thani, the jumping off point for the island of Koh Samui. Just prior to rumbling through the town of Thung Song was a newly constructed Buddhist temple with what I'm sure is one of the biggest statues in the country. It is the Big Nun. Dressed in the traditional white garb of the nuns of the Buddhist faith this statue stands out in the landscape and is flanked by smaller sculptures, a little like a Thai Snow White and the Seven Dwarfs. Eventually, I expect to see a drive-through McDonalds constructed beside the temple.

I took a taxi the 14 kilometres from the train station at Phum Pin to Surat Thani. On the way, I spoke with a retired American named Roger who'd been living on Koh Samui for the previous four months on his Australian pension.

"Australian pension?" I queried.

"Yeah, I came to Australia in 1979 and went to work among the Aborigines up around Cape York. I became an Australian citizen and when I retired I decided to come and live here in Thailand," he explained.

"I have a bungalow right on the beach and living on the island is not expensive," he said, making the whole idea sound quite appealing. It conjured up visions of banana cocktails sipped while reclining in a hammock as the sun slipped slowly beneath the horizon.

After staying overnight in Surat Thani, I travelled to Koh Samui via the express boat and found cheap accommodation in a bungalow right on the beach in the north. From my door to the beach took all of four steps, the water just eight or nine steps. Just across the water was the island of Koh Phangan. The water is so shallow I was almost halfway to Koh Phangan before it reached my neck.

There are three main waterfalls on the island with Na Muang Number Two the best of them. It is 80 metres above sea level and to get there involves a 30-40-minute hike through the bush.

Louis, an original Koh Samuian with a less than original Koh Samuian name, told me he'd carved out the track leading to the waterfall. Louis ran a small food and drink operation at the start of the long trek to the falls. It is hardly an easy walking path; very much find your footholds and watch your step.

In the process of walking to the waterfall, I passed by what is likely to become a shrine to the great God of Clear Plastic Water Bottles. A few years ago, someone discarded an empty plastic water bottle and others have since decided this particular spot was a good place to drop their finished bottles. Gradually a veritable mountain of clear, empty, plastic water bottles collected at this site. Perhaps 50 years from now the plastic water bottle mountain might become a tourist attraction in its own right and some weird Jim Jones-like cult may make Koh Samui its spiritual home.

***

I left Koh Samui via an ageing, ponderous rust-bucket of a car ferry and booked a Second-Class berth on the overnight sleeper train to Bangkok. This experience converted me into a train addict. Being able to order food whenever you felt like it and then being able to lie down on a thin but acceptable mattress made me think this was the way to travel.

Just after 5:00 a.m., we were roused out of our beds as the train lumbered into the capital. The sun had not yet put in an appearance but already the infamous Bangkok traffic had begun its build up.

At Hualumphong Station, I boarded the Third Class train to Ayutthaya, the Thai capital until the Burmese sacked it in 1767. Strolling out of my cheap hotel I met Anan, tuk-tuk driver and self-appointed tourist guide extraordinaire. Despite the dilapidated state of his little tuk-tuk, he spoke excellent English and suggested he take me to a good place for breakfast ("no charge for taxi") and I could make up my mind whether to take up his offer to be my tourist guide. To help convince me he produced a thick notebook in which the comments of previous victims, sorry, tourists were inscribed. Anan might have been a used car salesman in a previous life because he knew the value of word-of-mouth praise and written references in attempting to secure new business.

After breakfast, I told Anan I would take the tour and we proceeded to see every worthwhile chedi, stupa and Wat. After just over four hours with the interesting and very accommodating Anan, I really didn't know Wat was Wat. I took my leave of him, but not before he asked me to write a personal endorsement in his ever-expanding notebook and relieved me of our agreed 500 baht. It was money well spent.

***

Going for an ice cream in a local supermarket-department store, I noticed among the goods for sale was a selection of medals and ribbons that those who sport uniforms of all types (soldiers, police, traffic cops, security guards, hotel staff, parking attendants, lavatory cleaners) are wont to attach.

Every job worth its salt comes complete with a uniform. Rarely simple affairs, they are usually of a style to make the wearer look like an Admiral or an Air Chief Marshal.

Take car park attendants. Many places employ people to watch over the cars and motorbikes that may be parked outside a hotel. The old Anzac Hotel employed a young man to watch the bikes parked outside its premises at night. This man wore a white uniform, complete with peaked cap, whistle (an absolutely essential item for a job of this nature) and a row of medals attached to his chest.

The car park attendants at the Mike Shopping Mall wear a light brown uniform with peaked cap, whistle (which never seem to leave their mouths), lanyard and a row of medals adorning the chest. The security man at Tesco-Lotus probably received one of his medals for a stirring action against a sea of shopping trolleys.

***

On one occasion after leaving Thailand, I had an unscheduled stopover in Singapore. Two of the four toilets designed to relieve the economy-class passengers had somehow gone on the blink and the captain, rather than face the mutinous rumblings of overstressed bowels, diverted the plane to Singapore to undergo the unblocking of the drains or whatever it was that caused the things to seize up in the first place.

All the passengers trooped off the aircraft and we were able to wander around the transit area of Changi airport.

'Opulent' was the word which immediately sprang to mind to describe the transit area. Opulent in a Las Vegas casino kind of way. Two artificial waterfalls backlit with neon lights, a prayer room for the ethereally religious while the usual duty-free shops and bars were supplied for the more mundane. The area was staffed by a variety of mainly Chinese or Indian-looking employees, rather than ethnic Malays.

The toilets came complete with a 'Washroom Hygiene Inspection Card' attached to the door, "for your convenience". It purported to indicate just how regularly the bog was cleaned.

Changi airport smelt like it would be sacrilege to fart in it; Bangkok's Don Muang on the other hand smelt as if everyone considered it a rite of passage to fart in it.

After a delay of just over an hour, the conveniences in our metal hotel were back in full working order and we returned to the plane, feeling mighty relieved. Entering the lounge I noticed a sign that read, in part, '...passengers are advised to remove the following items...for safe custody...All firearms and ammunition...all explosives, incendiary devices and fireworks...' I didn't think your average garden-variety hijacker would quiver in his boots reading this and immediately surrender his firearms and explosives to 'safe custody.'

Laos: Between a Rock and a Hard Place

One of my trips to Thailand was combined with a trip north to the People's Democratic Republic of Laos for talks with government officials about making a documentary film on the problem of unexploded ordnance.

Many people were aware of the major land mines problem in nearby Cambodia, which claimed lives and maimed villagers every day, but not many were aware of the vast amount of lethal unexploded materiel littering the plains and valleys of Laos, destroying lives since 1964.

During the Second Indochina War (1964-1975), the United States dropped the equivalent of one tonne of bombs per capita on Laos in an effort to block North Vietnamese munitions and troop reinforcements moving down the Ho Chi Minh Trail. The bombing failed and the aerial campaign moved further inland and struck the Plain of Jars. Bombing ceased in 1973 but an estimated 20 percent of the ordnance had failed to explode and now just lay in wait for an unwary child or woman or peasant farmer to trigger the deadly mechanism.

I had received permission from the Lao government to make a film about the problem and was also in contact with the British Mines Advisory Group (MAG), one of the few organisations helping to remove the unexploded bombs.

I took the overnight sleeper train to the northern town of Nong Khai, pulling into the station just after 8:00 a.m. I took a songthaew to the border and, without a visa, went through the Thai border post and caught a bus across the Friendship Bridge to the Lao side.

This was where the real fun started.

8:30 a.m.: A polite Lao border official told me I needed $50 or 2,000 baht to cross into the country. No other money was accepted. I told them I had Australian money as well as about 1,000 baht. They said it was not good enough. Thinking I'd still be able to con my way into the country, I showed them letters from the Lao embassy in Canberra. The official told me to wait.

9:00 a.m.: I was allowed to pass through the border post with an official named 'L'- but only to make phone calls to other officials in the Lao capital, Vientiane. There was no answer- Lao officials didn't tend to start work too early.

9:10 a.m.: I phoned John Humphries, the main man at the British Mines Advisory Group (MAG). He said he was going to be out of town for the next 10 days and gave me another Foreign Ministry number to call.

9:20 a.m.: At that number, I spoke to a man who knew about me but could not authorise my entry into Laos. He asked me to ring back 10 minutes later.

9:40 a.m.: I rang the Foreign Ministry official again but he still couldn't give me a firm answer.

10:00 a.m.: 'L' took me upstairs to the Immigration office cafeteria where I was given a small meal of chicken and rice.

10:30 a.m.: I rang the Foreign Ministry official again. He was apologetic but said, "I'm sorry. You will have to pay."

10:40 a.m.: 'L' told me to catch a bus back across the Friendship Bridge and into Thailand. "Go to the bank in Nong Khai, change the baht and come back." It was to prove easier said than done.

10:45 a.m.: The returning bus was full and I found a tight spot right on the front step, but the door wouldn't close. Suddenly the compressor released the door and it slammed against my head. Cries of "oooh" emanated from the multitude inside the bus but it didn't hurt. No brain, no pain!

10:50 a.m.: I arrived back at the Thai border post and filled in the Immigration form.

10:55 a.m.: "Where is your Lao visa?" asked the Thai official at the border post.

"I didn't get one, I couldn't get into Laos," I replied.

"You have to go back to Laos and get a visa."

"I can't get one."

"You cannot come into Thailand."

Catch 22: Without a Lao exit visa, I couldn't enter Thailand, but without money, I couldn't get into Laos.

I walked away from the window, waited until his back was turned and then sneaked in anyway, catching a songthaew into Nong Khai. I was now illegally in Thailand.

11:20 a.m.: I collected 5,000 baht from my Visa card. Unfortunately, the girl damaged the hologram on the card so I requested a further 5,000 baht in case of future problems. I'd need to replace the card.

11:50 a.m.: Back at the Thai border post the Immigration officer (a different one) looked at my passport and said, "Where is your Thai entry stamp?" I told him what happened and, thankfully, he understood (it was obviously not a unique occurrence) and waved me through.

12:05 p.m.: Caught a bus across the bridge yet again and at the Lao border paid the 2,000 baht for my entry visa.

12:20 p.m.: Yet one more problem arose. My mate 'L', having already made a 300-400 baht profit on the exchange rate, told me I had to pay another 50 baht.

"For what?" I asked indignantly.

"For pass through is 20 baht and overtime is 30 baht," he replied.

"Overtime? What do you mean overtime? Get me the boss and we'll see about this," I was not impressed.

"OK, OK, you pay 20 baht and I pay the 30 baht."

We went to see the head Immigration official and he confirmed the extra fee. I paid the 20 and 'L' coughed up the 30 baht.

I found out later I had not been shaken down; 'L' was right about the overtime. They were the rules and he hadn't been trying to add to his 'take'.

12:40 p.m.: Found a songthaew and I was on my way to Vientiane at last.

I checked in to the Lani Guest House No 1. The room was air-conditioned, had a hot water shower but an uncomfortable double rattan-style bed more suited to a prison cell than a guesthouse. Nonetheless, the surroundings were idyllic. It was an old mansion dating from the French colonial era with high ceilings and plenty of teak wood furnishings. There were many such edifices around Vientiane, some in varying states of disrepair, others lovingly restored.

I ventured to the Ministry of Foreign Affairs and Culture and Information, a huge, white-painted building; a rabbit-warren of offices, manned by two or three people, huge ceilings, lazy fans, drab light-green faded paint work and laminated floor tiles- dull grey and well worn.

Brown wood desks, the kind you see in second-hand stores, or discarded at the tip, formed the bulk of the furniture. Most had a blue material covering to save them from dust.

I spoke with Som Detvongsa who told me to return at the next morning at 9:00 a.m. when I could see the appropriate officials and discuss my requirements for the documentary.

Red dust is one of my lingering memories of this lovely, somewhat run-down city, if city is really the word. The dust was everywhere, caking shoes and socks and rising up in little eddies at every gust of wind or with the passing of heavy vehicles. Still, it was better the dust, than the red mud it became after a decent spot of rain.

Up Lan Xang Avenue is the Pratuxai Gate, modelled on the Arc-de-Triomphe in Paris and built in 1969 with a load of American cement that had been meant for an extension of the Wattay airport runway. The U.S.-supported government thought it would add a nice touch to a victory celebration, once the enemy were defeated. Instead, it was to be the North Vietnamese-aided Pathet Lao who rumbled to victory in 1975

Potholes of varying sizes, designed to accommodate small bicycles or large trucks, were almost commonplace on the roads. On the pavement, it was a different ball game. Whole drainage covers were simply missing, exposing large black holes into which an inattentive person could easily fall, and maybe never be seen again. The danger to life, limb and dignity was increased at night due to poor street lighting. It became a case of approaching any darker-than-normal looking section of the pavement with extreme caution. I wouldn't recommend a casual stroll through the streets of Vientiane to anyone requiring a white stick.

The girls were some of the most attractive I have seen anywhere. They wore long ankle-length sarongs that showed off their shapely figures and I found the skirts very alluring. Most girls wore little or no make-up and came equipped with a ready smile.

I was surprised at the good English language skills of many people. I saw few beggars (probably all in re-education camps), while many Vietnamese or Chinese ran the businesses.

The following morning I moved into the Douangdeuane Hotel before going on to the Ministry of Foreign Affairs and Culture and Information. I arrived at 9:00 a.m. but was told the Director was going to be in a meeting until 10:00 a.m. I decided to wait and spent the time reading the *Vientiane Times* newspaper.

The Director turned up at 10:30 a.m. and, through an interpreter, I asked if I could have a Lao filmmaker named Som Ock work on the program with me and organise the camera, sound, and translator. I had come across Som Ock's name while flicking through the *Vientiane Times*. I reflected later on the vagaries of life. If the Director had not been in a meeting, I would never have seen the paper and not known of Som Ock.

***

Back at the hotel, I met an Australian expatriate named Humphrey. His real name was Greg and 'Humphrey' was a nickname he'd picked up during his 20 years of service in the Royal Australian Air Force. He was a nuggety character with a shaved head and moustache and, as I was to find out later, he liked a beer or 10.

He lived in Khon Kaen with his Thai wife and two young sons and was in Laos doing his visa run. He said he worked around the world on oilrigs; places like the Gulf of Mexico, the Faeroe Islands, and the Mediterranean.

He told me there was a train leaving Nong Khai for Khon Kaen at 12:30 p.m. the following Friday.

"It'll cost you about 35 baht and takes three hours to reach Khon Kaen," he said.

Humphrey then introduced me to his friend Simon, a former military intelligence man but now the Australian Military Attaché in Phnom Penh. He was also married to a Thai and used to live in Khon Kaen.

That afternoon I took a walk along the Mekong before sweeping out to the Pratuxai Gate again. On the way, I purchased half a bagatelle for 100 kip, and had a meal of fried chicken and ginger for 2,500 kip.

I paid 200 kip at the Gate for the right to take the stairs to the top, admired the sweeping vista of dusty thoroughfares and went on to That Luang, the most famous Buddhist temple in Vientiane.

By the time I walked back to the hotel I had worked up a decent appetite and went in search of culinary delights. I wandered to the end of the street and opposite the Mekong, I found John's restaurant.

A restaurant named John's intrigued me, so I stopped and spoke with the girl who ran the place.

She said her name was John (and that was how she spelt it), she was 24, had never been married nor even had a boyfriend. John told me she was the eldest of seven children; the youngest was a girl of nine. She worked from 7:00 a.m. until about 11:30 p.m. seven days a week and learnt English by listening and talking to foreigners who came in to the restaurant.

John said her family moved from Pakse 19 years earlier, she spent nine years in school and then worked for 18 months at the Tai-Pan Hotel in Vientiane. Her younger sisters still attended school from 8:00 a.m. until midday and again from 2:00 p.m. to 4:30 p.m.

John told me she had people from England, Denmark, Germany, and America write her letters, but she never replied so they soon stopped. I asked her why she never replied. "I didn't see the point. Most of these people I would probably never see again," she said, without malice.

She continued, "I'd like to have a boyfriend, but for a long time, not a short time. I would like to be married by the time I'm 25." (Considering her shop was gone the next time I came to Vientiane, maybe she managed to get her wish.)

After a good dinner, I walked along the riverfront and at the end of the reasonably well-lit area, I turned into a side street and came across a sparse looking bar with just two girls inside.

I sat down and ordered a bottle of Beer Lao. One of the girls came over and sat with me. She didn't speak a word of English and very little Thai. Her name was Bungan, she was 21-years-old and came from Sam Neua province, the former stronghold of the Pathet Lao during the Second Indochina War. Bungan said she'd been working in Vientiane for the past two years because there was no work in Sam Neua.

I left that bar and went to the nightclub situated next to the Saysonara Hotel. I no sooner sat down in a booth by myself than a Vietnamese man named Dao came over and asked if I would like to join his table. There were two other men at his table as well as three Lao taxi dancers. One of the men was supposedly the Chief of Customs in Vientiane; he was tall and thin, looked to be in his late forties, and was extremely drunk.

Dao told me he left what was then South Vietnam in 1972 for the United States before moving to Vientiane 18 months earlier. He had acquired a very pronounced American accent and asked if I would like a girl to come and sit with me. I said, "why not" and he sent his own girl to bring someone over.

Her name was Ae and she was just 17. She couldn't speak English but understood Thai and told me she had one older brother and five younger sisters. She lived with another taxi girl about 30 minutes out of town in a place costing about 300,000 kip a year. She said she earned about 60,000 kip a month in the bar. Ae later told me she'd slept with five Lao men in the four months she'd been working. At the end of the night Ae removed a ring from her finger and asked if I would come back to see her the following night. I hoped this wasn't some form of Lao marriage ceremony.

Dao, with his girl and his friend, gave me a lift back to my hotel in his pick-up truck. First, we followed the drunken Customs man- who insisted on climbing aboard his motorbike to ride home- to make sure he made it in one piece. Although he wobbled and weaved, he managed to make it without disappearing down one of Vientiane's rampant potholes.

After breakfast in the hotel the next morning, I met with Alain, a French-Canadian filmmaker, and his Lao assistant, in the hotel lobby. Alain had lived in Bangkok for five years and been in Vientiane for the previous two. He was going to Madagascar a few days after I spoke with him for a three-month stint to make a film with non-governmental organisation (NGO) funding. We chatted about the documentary and arranged to meet with Som Ock the next day.

In the early afternoon I walked to the Red Cross headquarters and asked for the location of the British Mines Advisory Group (MAG). At the time, a Laotian man working for the UNDP was delivering some papers to the Red Cross and he offered to take me close to the MAG headquarters in his white Toyota four-wheel drive. It was a beautifully air-conditioned vehicle I'm sure had never seen anything other than a Vientiane dirt road.

A Welshman working as a teacher at the UNDP gave me directions and I eventually found MAG headquarters in a roomy house in a side street. I spoke with Dianne Smith, an assistant to the Programme Director, who loaned me two videos about the unexploded ordnance problem.

I walked back towards the Mekong and while strolling along the waterfront I ran into the Welshman who had given me the directions to the MAG office. We had a beer together at an outside bar overlooking the Mekong. He had been contracted to teach English as a volunteer for two years and was 16 months into his stint.

"I live in a village just outside Vientiane which costs me nothing and I get 275 dollars a month," he told me.

He said courtship in Laos was something akin to living in the 1930s. "You know, mother comes along as chaperone. Even back in the days of the Vietnam War when Vientiane was full of brothels, the girls came mainly from Vietnam and Thailand," he said.

He continued, "For example in the village where I live there were a couple of attractive Lao girls who had had foreign boyfriends. The boyfriends have gone back to their homelands alone and now the girls are untouchable. The local men won't have anything to do with them and their only hope for marriage is to get another foreign boyfriend."

He then told me about a Lao girl and her elder brother- both orphans- who had been raised by Buddhist monks, who turned up on his doorstep one day.

"The brother could speak a little bit of English and he asked me to make his sister pregnant," he said.

"I said 'You mean marry her' and the brother said 'no, no, just give her babies'. She figured she'd done all right out of life even though she was an orphan and she thought she didn't need to be married," he concluded.

***

I went for dinner at John's place and met four American soldiers, who asked me to join them. Two of them told me they were in Laos for a holiday while another had been with the Unexploded Ordnance (UXO) program and was just finishing his tour of duty. The fourth was to be his replacement.

They explained to me that a treaty waiting to be signed in Oslo banning land mines did not cover the UXO type of material found in Laos and the reason for American opposition to this treaty was then President Bill Clinton did not want to tie the hands of the military.

One said, "American soldiers use claymore anti-personnel mines to secure a perimeter and then remove them when they move on."

They also bemoaned the fact the-then Senate and Congress contained just 17 percent of ex-service personnel whereas around 1970 the figure was approximately 70 to 80 percent.

"Many of them have never been outside the States. Some only make their first trip when they get elected. And these guys are enacting legislation which impacts on other countries."

After the Americans left, I asked John if I could watch the two videos I had on loan from MAG. In company with John, her father, his nephew, her young sister, and her cousin, we sat through *Inside Story: The Forgotten War*, an ATV US production.

It was interesting to watch this collection of different generations watch a documentary in English (a language they didn't understand), very quietly, very respectfully and with the occasional nodding of the head.

After taking the videos back to my hotel room, I kept my promise, wandered down to the Saysonara Hotel, and met up for a drink with Ae.

***

The next day I saw Humphrey before he returned to Khon Kaen and agreed to meet him on the coming Friday.

Alain picked me up and we went to meet Som Ock, sitting and drinking coffee in the patisserie next door to his office. Our discussions were fruitful and we agreed to a joint project, as long as I could get the funding from somewhere.

After we parted I went around to the *Discover Laos* magazine, met the Lao owner and Donald Ronk, the personable American editor. A tall, grey-haired, mustachioed, fifty-plus leather-skinned chain smoker, Don said he'd spent the last five years in Vientiane but had been around southeast Asia for most of the previous 30 years. He told me there had been a number of problems with *Discover Laos* magazine and the next issue, if any, would probably be his, and the magazines', last.

I met up with Don later in the day outside the Scandinavian Bakehouse, opposite Nam-Phu. Don said he used to edit *Asia Magazine* in Hong Kong and had worked on the *Bangkok Post*. He said he had enough money not to have to work any more. "Some people see me sitting here and think I'm the CIA station chief, either that or they think I'm a bum." I thought the only difference was around $50,000 a year.

"This is the most heavily-aided country, per capita, in the world. A lot of NGO's are really wasting enormous amounts of that aid money," Don said.

He continued, "I have an English friend who's getting paid $3,000 a month by AusAID for the next 12 months to sort out a report which they should already have completed. He is a computer type who goes in when NGO contracts are nearly up and fixes up the mess. Wherever there is aid money there are jobs for English speakers with qualifications, or even without qualifications."

Despite submissions to the Special Broadcasting Service (S.B.S.), the Australian Broadcasting Commission (A.B.C.) and even the Canadian Film Board through the auspices of Lloyd Axworthy, the Canadian Foreign Minister who had been one of the primary influences behind the Oslo agreement, I was never able to obtain the funding needed to produce the documentary.

***

On the Friday morning, I checked out of the hotel, and took a 45-minute ride by tuk-tuk to the Friendship Bridge. Leaving Laos and returning to Thailand proved far easier than my experience of a few days before and I caught the 12:30 p.m. train from Nong Khai to Khon Kaen. Humphrey and his two kids, Chatchi and Jesse, met me at the railway station. Humphrey also picked up another Australian, a guy named Dave, who was on his way back to Bangkok after spending a few days in Laos.

We went back to Humphrey's place, a two-storey affair in an estate complex and met his wife Nang. After drinking copious quantities of Beer Lao, Humphrey took us into town and we checked into the plush Kosa Hotel. With a discount Humphrey helped to arrange, I paid just over 1,000 baht a night for a room as plush as the room I had stayed in three years earlier in the Fortune Hotel in Bangkok. It just happened to be a good deal cheaper.

Next door to the hotel was a massage parlour, or 'goldfish bowl', one of three in Khon Kaen. After having a drink and a look at the girls, we had dinner and then Humphrey took us to the most popular of the 'goldfish bowls'.

The girls charged 900 baht for 90 minutes. I asked a beautiful girl in a long black dress to sit with us. Her name was Nang, she was 24-years-old and came originally from Uborn. She spoke Khmer as well as Thai and had been working for three years in Khon Kaen. She was the third of four sisters; the elder pair had married Thai men.

Nang had never been married and had no children. She lived out of town with a girlfriend and claimed not to have a boyfriend at the time. She worked from 6:00 p.m. until midnight five or six days a week and saw an average of two or three clients a day. She'd been to Pattaya but told me she wouldn't work there, "too many Arabs, cocaine and heroin."

***

The next morning, Humphrey took Dave and myself to the train station and we purchased two Third Class tickets for the seven and a half hour trip back to Bangkok.

We passed through flat rolling country, with seas of verdant green paddy interspersed with clumps of gum and mango trees, flanked on occasion by high limestone peaks; the weather was overcast with occasional drizzle.

In a fruitless exercise designed to improve cleanliness, the Bangkok city fathers introduced a 2,000 baht on-the-spot-fine for people caught littering. Sadly, old habits die hard. I was walking with a girl in Lumpini Park one day when we purchased two bottles of cold drinking water. After unscrewing the top from her bottle, she carelessly flung the lid to the ground, not two metres away from a rubbish bin. When I chastised her for this, she smiled and replied, "But it's only small, it doesn't matter."

On our train trip from Khon Kaen to Bangkok, the crowd grew thicker and thicker at each stop until it was standing room only our carriage. The chicken and sticky rice hawkers as well as the fruit and drink sellers changed from stop to stop.

A young Thai man sitting opposite us threw all his rubbish out the window, while I disposed of mine on the floor. He looked at me and pointed at a sign, written in Thai, which must have stated something like, 'don't discard your rubbish on the train as we can't be bothered to have people clean them.' I tried to explain it was better if the garbage remained on the train so it could be cleaned up later and taken away, rather than be cast out the window to pollute the countryside.

"But if you leave on the train you can have 2,000 baht fine," he replied. Therefore, the fine applied not just to the streets of Bangkok but the floors of trains and yet not, so it seemed, to the beautiful countryside we traversed.

Along major thoroughfares throughout the kingdom, a small army of underpaid people, mainly women, spend their long working days bedecked in brightly coloured clothing that usually covers them from head to foot. As protection from the sun, they wear a straw hat, sometimes of the conical variety. A scarf to keep out the dust of the road and the smell of the traffic usually covers their brown faces, and only their eyes are visible. Armed with straw brooms, their job description seems to be to move the accumulated dust and debris of the city streets from one part of the road to another part of the road. When it rains, they use their brooms to move the rapidly stagnating water to a position where it can stagnate more appropriately. I suppose if people stopped littering their onerous job would be made so much easier.

Thailand's population numbers well above 60 million people. While Bangkok may contain up to 20 percent or more, the vast majority still remain in rural areas. Scenes like this are commonplace throughout southeast Asia.

Rice planting and harvesting requires long hours in the heat of the day; the financial rewards for most farmers are limited. It's hardly surprising that so many young women find their way into the bar scene.

Nuremburg Rallies come to Chiang Mai

On my first visit to the northern Thai city of Chiang Mai, I brought along a lady named Tik. She worked in a karaoke bar and was a friend of some Thai people I knew in Australia. Tik was 32-years-old, quite tall with the pale skin so admired by Thais, a small mouth and curvaceous figure. When I met her for the first time, in the bar, Tik was wearing a pink micro mini with an open back. All the other 30 or so girls working in the bar wore similar very short skirts and dresses of various hues. The gear was very garish, almost gay, with lots of baubles, bangles and beads. Tik had a 13-year-old daughter and had been working at this particular bar for three years.

Each of the girls and the four men who worked there took turns at going on-stage and singing. When their girl got up to sing she would be rewarded with tips from her hopeful paramour. The admirer would send a tip (a minimum of 100 baht) attached to a garland of flowers. A flunky would go to the front of the stage and place the garland with the money attached around the recipient's neck. She would then *wai* her thanks while continuing to sing.

Tik earned 3,000 baht a month for working at the bar. The bar was open from 7:00 p.m. until 3:00 a.m. and each person would sing about four songs a night, or one every two hours or so; hardly back-breaking work.

She had never been to the picturesque northern city and accepted my invitation quite readily.

At Hualumphong Station, I booked the train tickets and then decided to test out the availability of accommodation in Chiang Mai by going into the tourist information office in the station.

The lady behind the counter recommended the Felix City Inn as a good place and, surprise, surprise, if I booked now she could offer me a substantial discount on the normal rate. I found out later the large discount was really nothing of the sort; I was saving at best a couple of hundred baht a night.

I also asked about checkout times and was told it was midday. As I was going to book the 4:40 p.m. train from Chiang Mai, I didn't want to waste over four hours carting my luggage around, so I paid for an extra night. Imagine my surprise when I read a notice in the hotel indicating I could have availed myself of a late checkout at 3:00 p.m.

On board the train, the compartment was quite full and one of our neighbours was a French backpacker with his Thai girlfriend (who conversed with him in fluent French). In the opposite compartment was a German man with a Thai girl who conversed easily with him in German. It was a strange feeling listening to two Thai ladies converse in two separate European languages while riding a train in Thailand.

The next morning, as the train was approaching Chiang Mai, I spoke with the French backpacker. He told me he was from the French-speaking part of Switzerland and his girlfriend, originally from Laos, had lived in Switzerland for over 20 years.

At the station, we were met by a contract driver who delivered us to Felix City Inn after first dropping off a few other passengers to less salubrious, yet no doubt cheaper, digs. The Inn is located inside the old walled city, a modern-looking building with a wide foyer and restaurant. Floor-to-ceiling windows meant you could sit and read the newspaper and watch any passing parade; not that much seemed to happen in the street outside.

The hotel rooms were brown. Brown walls, brown carpets, brown bed coverings. Brown, in varying shades, seemed to be the preferred colour of the Felix City Inn.

After breakfast, I went in search of the English Department at the Chiang Mai University to see a man named Graham Enwright.

After arriving at the one of the administrative buildings, I spoke with a lady who made a couple of phone calls to ascertain his whereabouts. A pair of political science students graciously gave me a lift in their car to the Department.

The cars belonging to students were numerous and parking was hard to find with vehicles parked across and in front of others. Not a single car looked over 10 years old although I did spot a student in a 20-year-old Mercedes.

While I waited for Graham to finish his class I chatted with an Italian photojournalist named Frederico- he said he was on assignment for an Italian magazine to photograph Chiang Mai, the university, the Buddhist temple at Doi Suttep, and the nightlife.

I met Graham, a thin Englishman in later middle age, with grey hair, moustache and a pleasant manner. He ran an organisation called the Patcharaporn Thai Education Fund and it was this I had come to talk about.

The Fund was, in the words of its founder, "a small personal effort, in memory of a young Thai girl's untimely death." The story surrounding the founding of the Fund would make a suitable plot for a Hollywood movie.

The Patcharaporn Thai Education Fund was established in 1988 to provide the financial support needed to educate girls from poor families and give them a chance at a wider choice of careers.

Graham said the fund was not a registered charity in either England or Thailand. He received money from a Singapore Trust Fund that paid for most of the girls, who were housed in a dormitory. He paid everyday expenses out of his own pocket.

In England, he explained, the cost of registration of a charity was prohibitive in England and in Thailand, as a foreigner, he could only control 49 percent. Graham adheres to a no-expenses policy with the Fund and handing 51 percent control of the charity to the Thais would mean he could not guarantee the rigid no-expense rule.

"I've seen what can happen when the Thais get their hands on something like this. They can milk it for all it is worth and do no good at all," he said.

Our conversation continued for some time and I began to wish I had an extra day to spend in Chiang Mai to see more of what Graham was doing.

That night, at around 3:00 a.m. I was woken by a loud buzzing noise emanating from the bathroom. It sounded like a blowfly on amphetamines had become entrapped in the fluorescent light area of the bathroom and was trying to alert the world to its plight. The noise continued for ages and then suddenly stopped.

Ten minutes later, it started again and, unable to sleep, I rang reception and informed them of the noise. They immediately changed our room; I suspected this was an on-going problem with this room at the hotel. The noise was quite audible from the hallway.

Unfortunately, at about 5:30 a.m. I was again roused from my slumbers by what sounded like a cross between the Nuremberg Rallies and an Evangelists' Convention- or at least a Thai version of the same. A booming Hitlerian-like voice led a series of chant-like songs, although at first I couldn't discern whether the language was Thai, English, or some ancient tongue lost to the mists of time. A few speeches, at peak volume, thundered into the room, peppered with rare silences until the assault on the senses thankfully ceased around 7:00 a.m.

As it turned out the mob responsible for this cacophony was a Thai Christian fundamentalist organisation. They had taken over the fourth-floor function room to conduct their services and annoy the bejesus out of everyone else. I only found out about their in the hotel when I asked the reception at breakfast if there was a Christian Church in the vicinity.

"No, sir," was the reply. "Why do you ask?"

"Because very early this morning I was awoken by a lot of singing and chanting," I replied.

"Oh, that is the Christians. They are on the fourth floor," she informed me with a smile.

I decided to go upstairs and look at the fourth floor. Inside the brown walls of the function room were about 100 of the faithful seated at a number of long tables. A short, bald, bespectacled character, whose head and shoulders barely cleared the rostrum from whence he preached, led the chanting.

Later that morning we went by tuk-tuk to the railway station to book tickets for the return journey to Bangkok. Sitting in the back of the tuk-tuk, I was amused to read a notice stuck to the roof of the vehicle that read: *'The driver of this bus was trained. You will be serviced in a standard manner with safety.'*

That night I took a walk by myself along the Thepae gate region and was propositioned by a *katoey* on a motorbike offering me a massage for 200 baht. I politely declined.

That night, Tik and I went to the Winter Festival market in Salaglong, 15 minutes by tuk-tuk from the hotel. The Winter Festival was like an amusement park after an explosion. A giant Ferris wheel bedecked with little white lights dominated the landscape and around it wound a long steam train. A Thai country-rock band and Muay-Thai boxing competed for attention with a snake show, while a multitude of stalls sold everything from T-shirts, shorts and hill-tribe garments to jackets, silks, and toys. The complex was spread over a wide area and lit up like a Christmas tree. The majority of Thais were sensibly dressed in jackets and coats against the bitter winter chill of 14 degrees Celsius.

Unfortunately, just after 5:00 a.m. the Herald Angels mob, unconcerned about such mundane Christian principles as consideration for others, once again began their wailing, chanting, singing, and general raving from the fourth-floor function room.

I rang the front desk but was told the noise couldn't be halted and the manager would not be in until 10:00 a.m. I bet he didn't sleep in the hotel.

"This is their last time, sir," was the girl's answer.

"Yes, it's also my last night here," I replied.

Later that morning when I went to pay my bill, the receptionist asked, "What do you think of my hotel?"

Of course, she was expecting me to give it glowing marks and my response of, "Not much," brought a surprised look to her face.

I explained about the successive early morning disturbances of the Christian fundamentalists and she replied, "Next time you come they probably not here."

"Next time I come," I said. "I probably not here."

Cambodia: Year Zero Plus 25

Early in 2000, I went on a visa run to Phnom Penh, the capital of a Cambodia that was finally, after more than two decades, basking in an uneasy sort of internal peace. It was very similar to Vientiane except it was perhaps a more vibrant and interesting city, certainly bigger in area and population.

Like Vientiane, there were no real high-rises in Phnom Penh and the old colonial French influence was still obvious, in spite of the Pol Pot years. The main boulevards were wide and well paved but the side streets were full of potholes, so motorbikes were forced to zigzag and a short trip became akin to a motocross rally.

Motorbikes were in abundance, as were cyclos, and I even saw the odd pony-drawn cart. Some women walked gracefully with platters of food balanced precariously on their heads. People told fortunes at night by candlelight seated at tiny trestle tables along Sisowath Quay, a promenade running alongside the Tonle River, a tributary of the mighty Mekong.

Military police dressed in fatigues or just drab khaki travelled around in pairs on motorbikes with AK-47's strapped across their shoulders. Ordinary police and sometimes soldiers skulked at intersections.

One of the ways people make a living is by acting as tour guides, taking those who hire them by motorbike out and about the city and surrounding countryside.

Although I generally like to do my own sightseeing, I picked one moto (as the motorcycle riders are colloquially known) and offered him the princely sum of five dollars a day to take me out and about.

Tool Kok, as onomatopoeic a word as Bangkok, is a rutted street on the outskirts of the northern part of Phnom

Penh with wooden shanties where the cheapest of the Vietnamese and Cambodian prostitutes ply their trade. It seemed a little incongruous to me that the headquarters of Funcinpec, the political party led by Prince Norodom Ranaridh, was situated right on the corner of the street.

The police had supposedly closed down the area and many of the shacks did indeed look unoccupied. Nevertheless, there were plenty of girls shouting out to me as I went past with my moto man.

We stopped outside one place and a couple of the girls came up. The moto asked how much to go back with me to my hotel. The boss was quickly on the scene and he asked 40 dollars. Considering I had been told the girls in Tool Kok were supposed to be the cheapest in town, it was obvious the boss was taking advantage of my 'green-horn' status.

The whole street was shabby and dirty and certainly didn't fill me with any lusty desires. Nor did the majority of the girls I saw. Not one looked comparable with the beer bar girls and go-go dancers of Pattaya and Bangkok.

Street 63 is home to massage parlours, again mainly stocked with Vietnamese girls. An Australian man who spends six months of the year teaching in Phnom Penh told me most of the girls are in Cambodia illegally and if caught out walking by the military police are liable to be whisked off into the countryside where, as he put it, they "become live dartboards for the soldiers in the camps. Of course they're never seen again and are probably fucked to death."

Chhouk Tep Karaoke Bar is one of a number of bars around the city where prostitutes congregate. Places like Martini's (closed in 2004) and Sharky's were also noted for their working girls.

One night Moto- as I took to calling him- and I went to Chhouk Tep and the place was so dark I thought the owners had forgotten to pay the electricity bill. We were ushered to a table near the dance floor and ordered a couple of beers. The amber liquid tasted like the last emission of a dying water buffalo. I thought Singha was a bit rough, but this stuff was truly awful.

Svay Pak, also known as K-XI, is situated about 11 kilometres outside of Phnom Penh, and is a popular destination for locals and tourists looking for sex. One night I went with Moto and, after travelling for around 15 minutes along the darkened roadway, we turned off the main road into a short rutted street alongside which were a number of buildings housing the working girls. They were mainly Vietnamese and called out to us to stop and come inside.

Instead, Moto went to the end of the street and stopped opposite a place where the sliding metal doors were drawn. He called out and the door was opened about one metre to reveal a gaggle of girls congregated in the front room. He drove his motorcycle inside and the doors were quickly shut behind us.

The mamasan ushered me across the neatly tiled floor through a flimsy black curtain and down the hall and through a blue sheet that covered the entrance to another room. Inside were two four-seater black upholstered lounges backed against either wall and in the centre was a wooden table.

I sat down and within a minute, the sheet was pulled back and in stepped two obviously young Vietnamese girls who proceeded to come over and sit down, one on either side of me. The more experienced-looking girl began to mechanically massage my left leg while the other girl merely wrapped an arm about me.

Moto and the mamasan sat down opposite me. I asked how old the girls were and Moto replied, matter-of-factly, “14.”

“You can have them both if you want,” said Moto.

The more experienced of the two looked at me and said, “Good ‘yum-yum’.”

Moto laughed and said, “My friend Wolfgang took that one when he come here before. Very good ‘yum-yum’ he tell me.”

I was fairly sure I knew what he meant by ‘yum-yum’ but still asked, “What is ‘yum-yum’?”

Moto merely stuck a finger in his mouth and made a sucking noise. I got the picture.

I looked at the two girls and thought if I really wanted to have sex with them there wouldn’t be any hassle at all, and if I wanted the two at once that was also available.

I said to Moto, “How much for the girls?”

He questioned the mamasan and then replied, “70 dollars.”

I haggled and the price eventually came down to 50 dollars. From the beginning, I had no intention of taking them, either singly or as a double-act, having intentionally brought just 10 dollars with me. I wanted to get a handle on the prices they were asking.

“Have you got any older girls?” I asked.

Moto talked to the mamasan, she went out and came back a minute or so later with another two girls.

“How old are they?” I asked.

“15,” he replied, after asking the mamasan.

I was getting the strong impression they believed foreign men were only interested in really young girls, because of a fear of AIDS or because they liked young flesh.

“Haven’t you got someone around 18 or 19?” I asked.

Both Moto and the mamasan looked at me as if I was some kind of necrophiliac.

Moto spoke with the increasingly-frustrated mamasan who again departed, with the two 15-year-olds in tow while the 14-year-olds remained seated with me.

She came back with another two girls who turned out to be 17 and 19. At least that seemed a little more reasonable so I asked them to sit with me.

Neither could speak a word of English and so communication, such as it was, went through Moto to the mamasan and thence to the girls. Both were prepared to go with me and the price for a short time with the pair was going to be 50 dollars. This soon came down to 40 dollars and eventually to 20 dollars for just one girl.

While my negotiations were taking place, I could hear plenty happening outside as a number of Cambodian men came to the brothel and began taking the waiting girls.

I was fairly certain Moto, not surprisingly, had a slice of any action and that's why he had come to this particular place, but after I pretended to be apologetic and explained I only had 10 dollars on me, we left the premises.

In fact, according to reliable sources, the girls at K-XI go for five dollars a time, with three dollars going to the house and a lousy two dollars to the girl. The fact the mamasan and my Moto started the bidding at 10 times the going rate did not really surprise me. After all, I was a tourist who didn't speak a word of Khmer. I later learned that girls, children really, as young as four could be procured for sexual services in K-XI.

While I am hardly a prude, I found the scene sordid and somewhat pathetic. How anyone could possibly be sexually 'turned on' by places like Tool Kok and K-XI is beyond me. Then again, there are plenty of people who find the bar scene in Pattaya equally abhorrent and repulsive, so who am I to start moralising.

Welcome to Venus

Oscar Wilde once wrote, "Those who go beneath the surface do so at their own peril." It is a warning that seems particularly appropriate for foreigners who venture to Pattaya, for she is an ingénue whose ambiguity and ambivalent nature flicker like puppets in a shadow play.

It has been said trying to define the essence of Thailand is like trying to divide water with a fork. This enigmatic country can seduce or repel you; dazzle or dismay you; exhilarate or frustrate you, all at the same time.

After all, the 'never mind' phrase *'mai pen rai'*, is one of the reasons why Thailand is such a wonderful place; it is also one of the reasons why it can be so frustrating.

For example, Christmas, New Year's Eve, Chinese New Year, Songkran, and Loy Krathong are a licence to go crazy with fireworks. The sale of these weapons of mass explosion and noise is exceeded only by exuberance in their use. Anyone would think Pattaya had become a war zone at times, especially in the streets containing beer bars.

Walking down the *sois* becomes a matter of taking your future health into your hands as firecrackers the size of small bombs go off all around you; and the unwary may easily stumble into a bargirl ambush and find the artillery starting to find its range and landing uncomfortably close. Then again, I've spent an evening under the Eiffel Tower in Paris on the night before Bastille Day, and the French are equally adept at throwing firecrackers around in an almost random fashion. Admittedly, the Thai government began to crack down on the sale of these explosive devices after the turn of the century.

At these times, parties abound at the various bars and I've never seen so many unhappy looking pigs, all trussed up, and being roasted on spits. To be in Pattaya, especially between Christmas and New Year, and in the pork business would be the way to make a small fortune.

As with most things in life, there is no black and white in Thailand; when viewed through the kaleidoscopic menagerie of its ethnic diversity it comes out as a multitude of colours, and all of them grey.

The transition from courtesan to consort to marriage is a constant theme in the relationships between foreign men and Thai bargirls. The transition for the girl is very often based on 'face' (that very Asian of all emotions and akin to 'pride' in Westerners), and obligation. The Thai bargirl will save her own 'face' first and if she is to be taken from the bar by a man who will look after her she will generally treat him with respect and may even come to 'love' him. The fact he will take care of her makes her obligated to him, and most girls will honour that obligation.

A key mistake made by foreign men is mistaking lust for love (but that is typical of men anyway), and misunderstanding the depth of a bargirl's desire for a better life for herself, her children (of which most have at least one), and her family (which usually consists of parents, grandparents, aunts, uncles, a multitude of siblings, and their offspring). There are many tender and loving relationships that emerge out of the dregs of the bar scene, although sadly these seem to constitute the exception rather than the rule and are not necessarily the fault of the girl. With divorce statistics in many First World nations hovering around the 50 percent mark, and with many people choosing to stay in loveless relationships 'for the sake of the children', the failure rate among bargirl-foreigners might not be much worse.

There is a saying, 'you can take the girl out of the bar, but not the bar out of the girl'. Most people tend to blithely agree with the statement, however, a Thai lady who runs a number of establishments on Soi Cowboy in Bangkok told the free newspaper *Guide Of Bangkok,* "It's not true. We've got several families in our village where the girl's worked here and married a foreigner and they have a proper family life."

When I first became interested in Asian girls- and Thais in particular- I had a number of people, (mainly Australian women) ask if I was, "looking for a nice subservient little doormat." These people had never been to Thailand and had no idea of the potentially fiery nature of Thai women. A "doormat" is something a Thai woman- especially an ex-bargirl- would never be, no matter how much she loved her man. They are more than capable of getting physically violent if provoked to anger and, on more than one occasion, I have witnessed assaults between Thai women, and not just in Pattaya. Not for nothing is Thailand home to the best micro-surgeons in the world at re-attaching severed male appendages: when they can be retrieved from the beaks of ducks or the jaws of the local mongrel.

Prostitution is hardly light years away from the lives of the average person. My travels around the world have shown it to be quite clearly a fixture of the gender relations of most economically stratified societies, a place of ordinary people, leading less than ordinary lives.

Psychologists claim anybody exposed to prostitution over a lengthy period of time must suffer some emotional damage. How can anyone blame a bargirl in Bangkok or Pattaya for looking askance at each new foreigner, trying to determine his real motivations? After all the lies, the deceit, the fabrications, the false promises made in the heat of passion is it any wonder the longer a girl works in the sex industry the harder it is for each new man to reach down and touch her heart and soul. It's no wonder many take up with Thai men again when they recognise the cultural gap dividing them and foreign men is so wide.

An ex-bargirl in Australia told me, “You must look for a girl with not good English; not work long time.” Implicit in her remark was those girls who had mastered the *lingua franca* of the world of prostitution were beyond reach, their hearts being far too damaged to be mended.

One of the most effective ways of reducing the level of the sex trade is to give the urban and rural poor greater access to long-term education (up to university level) and improve social services.

The basic wage of around 160-200 baht a day is hardly an incentive for people to stay on the land or work long hours in factories. Allied to the low wages is the fact so many farming families have debts they can never hope to repay and those debts are likely to grow rather than diminish. To then criticise the girls who find themselves involved in the international sex trade, either within Thailand or overseas, is hardly beneficial. When people are not in a position to make reasonable lifestyle choices there is no point in Western do-gooders preaching and proclaiming lofty ideals. Preaching about the virtue of Western cultural mores does not put rice on the table.

Even so there are girls who have no qualms or inhibitions about what they are doing. They have healthy sexual appetites and, in the Thai tradition of sating the appetite, are quite content with what they do. Senator Mechai once commented that bargirls, “interpret sex differently, they believe sex to be an asset, not a liability.” After all, they generally only go with men they like, and the bonus is they get paid for it.

There was once a go-go bar named Venus and the girls who worked out the front would intone, “Hello sir, welcome to Venus...” Pattaya does have an out of this world feel; at least the barkers gave me some idea of its rightful place in the cosmos.

Thai people often ask as I prepare to leave the country, “When will you come back to Thailand?”

I cannot envisage ever uttering the word, “Never.”

Glossary of Terms

Baht-Bus: Correctly known as a 'songthaew' they are similar to the Jeepney in the Philippines. In Pattaya, they are painted dark blue, and numbered, and resemble a large covered utility with bench seats down either side of the rear tray. They pick up a multitude of passengers on a circuit that basically encompasses the Beach Road and Second Road.

Bar Fine: An amount of money paid by a customer to take a particular girl (or boy) out of a bar. The money goes to the bar owner although a part of it is later remitted to the girl. In a go-go bar the bar fine may vary from 400 up to 1,000 baht, although the norm is 500 baht. Of this amount, the girl will receive around 100 baht. In a beer bar, the bar fine is generally 200-400 baht. Of this, the girl will get between 20 and 50 baht.

Lady Drink: A customer might buy this drink for a girl working in a go-go or beer bar. In Bangkok, the Lady Drinks are usually about the same price as a drink for a customer but in Pattaya, they tend to be more expensive. In the go-go bars, a girl who sits with a customer will have a spiel that runs along the lines of: "hello, what your name?" (she will forget it in 30 seconds); "where you come from?" (like they know where the hell Australia is, or could care less); "Buy me dlink?" Now this is something they DO care about, because it is money in their pocket.

If you agree to buy a drink then, in some bars, a champagne flute half-filled with Pepsi will arrive for the girl. Some girls may have a few sips and rarely finish the drink.

The reason for this hard-sell approach is in many Bangkok bars the girls need to 'sell' 50 or more drinks a month to help keep their full salary. In Pattaya, they usually need around 30 drinks a month. Most Lady Drinks range in price from 70 to an expensive 130 or more baht, out of which the girl will receive between 20 and 60 baht. Most girls don't actually want a drink as such, just the money.

Long Time: This is where a girl agrees to stay all night with a customer, again for an agreed amount. With some girls, if they like the customer, they will stay long into the next day. With others, they will be up and out of the hotel room at the crack of dawn. Many girls, especially those on the lookout for a potential marriage partner, will try and stay with someone they like for as long as that person is on holiday, becoming more like a *mia chow* (rented wife). Of course, it is also advantageous in the sense they know they will have a regular income for a couple of weeks or perhaps longer. Equally, many girls don't want to have a multitude of partners, rightly fearful of STD's and AIDS.

Mamasan (also Mamasang): Originally a Japanese phrase, it equates with the Western term 'Madam', although the mamasan of a go-go bar rarely has a financial stake in the establishment. The mamasan is usually an ex-bargirl grown too old for the game or a girl hoping to better herself. There are also a number of 'toms'-butch lesbians who are easily spotted as they dress like men and have short-cropped hairstyles- who work as mamasans in Pattaya.

The mamasan usually has to be able to speak, read and write passable English, control the girls in her bar and be the conduit between them and the owner.

Sex Fee: Although not a specific term as such, it is different to a bar fine. This is the amount of money a girl will ask to be paid after agreeing to leave the bar with a customer. A customer, say in a go-go bar, pays the bar fine (see above) and will pay the girl an amount set by agreement with her, usually before leaving the bar. Some go-go girls ask for between 1,000 and 1,500 baht "short-time" and up to 3,000 baht for "all-night" or "long-time". Most beer bar girls will stay all night for between 500 and 1,000 baht. Strange as it may seem, many beer bar girls are far more attractive than their go-go counterparts and therefore represent better 'value', for want of a better term.

Short Time: Quite literally a girl will go with a customer for a short period of time, usually just long enough to go back to a customer's hotel (or upstairs to a short-time room), shower, have sex once, shower again and go, most of the time back to work. A dancer will talk a customer into going "short-time": the punter pays the bar fine and generally pays the girl between 500 and 1,500 baht. The "short-time" lasts anything up to an hour or more depending on the girl and the length of time it takes a customer to orgasm. The money for the bar fine is paid up-front, but the girl is only paid after sex.

Songthaew (see Baht Bus)

A Cynic's Guide to Bar Girl Speak

"Butterfly" (or, "you butterfly me)": If you so much as look at, or converse with, another female, be she a bargirl or otherwise, then you are liable to be labelled a "butterfly". That is someone who cannot be trusted and who will go with other women when your current lady is out of sight. Her excuse on the other hand for going with other men is "I work."

"Handsome man/ sexy man": Walking past most beer bars you will find girls calling out to you to come and sit down and have a drink. One of the best ways to attract people into the bar is to shout a line like "handsome man, come over here please". Flattery will get you everywhere and the Thai bargirls have the flattery game down pat. Depending whether it is high or low season, you may hear girls shout out "handsome man", "sexy man" or just "papa". In high season, only men they really think are attractive get a "handsome man" tag. Then it is "sexy man" or, the bottom of the pile, "papa". In low season, almost every man becomes "handsome" and "sexy", even the older men who a few months earlier might have been referred to as "papa".

"I don't like Thai man, boxing too much" (or "butterfly too much"): This phrase is used to indicate that although they may have one or two children to a Thai father, they no longer wish to associate with this allegedly vile version of the male species. Almost every bargirl in Pattaya will say they don't like Thai men. The truth is a large number of them have Thai boyfriends or husbands, especially those girls working in the go-go bars. On occasions, the boyfriend goes off to work in a Boys go-go bar (even though he is not gay) and the girl will go to work in a female go-go bar. They will meet up later in the night after their respective bars have closed.

The reasons they give for ostensibly not liking Thai men is they (the men) tend to go out drinking too much and will come home and bash them. A study conducted in a Bangkok slum found about half of the women were bashed regularly by their husbands.

Alternatively, the man will go out to bars and go with prostitutes or find a second girlfriend. Indeed the incidence of *mia noi,* or second wives, among the more wealthy and powerful Thais is such that it appears more common than uncommon.

Amongst Thai women, the men are notorious for being womanisers. Far greater than foreigners according to some women I have spoken to. An edition of the *Thai-Oz News* (a newspaper for the Thai community in Sydney) stated that a survey of foreign nationalities found Australian men were the least likely to be unfaithful to their wives. Whether true or not is probably immaterial. Perceptions form attitudes and opinions as much as reasoned argument and Thai women generally perceive their men to be largely unfaithful.

"I look for good man, good heart": With many girls this simply means someone we would all like: good-looking, athletic, kind, youthful (though not necessarily young) and- in the case of most girls- plenty of money to take care of her and her family. Of course the main desire is for a man with a large wallet rather than a large penis, and a good heart rather than good-looking.

"I see you first time, I love you": This phrase is used by some girls as a bit of a joke, but by others in a serious fashion designed to lure the unwary punter into thinking he has found his 'perfect match' without even trying. The whole idea is to flatter the intended victim so he will immediately decide to pay the bar fine and take her home.

"She not work today" or **"She not come work, she sick":** When you go to a bar and ask to see a particular girl you know and she has already been bar-fined by another man then it is likely the others will tell you it is her day off or she's called in sick and had to go home. In 99.99 percent of cases, this is a lie, but only a white lie designed to save the girl's face, and yours also, as well as getting you to come back another time.

"Up to you- your holiday": The almost standard response to a "what do you want to do?" question by a foreigner. Since the man is paying the bills, the girl will generally be whatever you want her to be for as long as you are willing to pay her. If you want to go riding elephants or looking at crocodiles at the local mini zoo, then she will too; if you want to go to Jomtien Beach and hire a jet ski, she will come also. If you want to sit and drink all day in a beer bar then she'll probably put up with that as well. You are paying her 'wages' and she is your 'employee'. For most girls you are nothing more than a walking wallet and she will stay with you for as long as you pay her.

AUSTRALIA'S
No.1
COMEDY
HIT!
PAUL HOGA
LIGHTNIN
JACK